BRICS: The Emergence of a New World Order

A Deep Analysis of the Five Emerging Powers - Brazil, Russia, India, China, and South Africa - and Their Impact on the Global Future

John BRICSington

1. **Introduction to the BRICS** • Definition and history of the BRICS (Brazil, Russia, India, China, South Africa).

2. **Economics of the BRICS** • Analysis of the economies of each member and their global impact.

3. **Politics of the BRICS** • Examination of the domestic and foreign policies of BRICS countries.

4. **International Relations** • Analysis of relations between the BRICS and other global actors.

5. **New World Order** • Definition and key concepts of the new world order.

6. **Impact of the BRICS on the New World Order** • How the BRICS are shaping the new world order.

7. **Technology and Innovation** • Role of the BRICS in technological development and innovation.

8. **Sustainable Development** • Policies and practices of sustainable development adopted by the BRICS.

9. **Inequalities and Disparities** • Examination of inequalities and disparities within and among BRICS countries.

10. **Conflicts and Cooperation** • Analysis of conflicts and areas of cooperation among BRICS members.

11. **Climate Change** • Role and responsibility of the BRICS in the context of climate change.

12. **Defense and Security Strategies** • Defense and security policies of the BRICS in the new world order.

13. **Culture and Society** • Impact of the cultures and societies of the BRICS on the world.

14. **Financial Institutions** • Role of BRICS financial institutions, such as the BRICS Bank.

15. **International Trade** • Analysis of the BRICS' role in international trade.

16. **Globalization vs. Nationalism** • Discussion on how the BRICS balance globalization and nationalism.

17. **Human Rights** • Analysis of the human rights situation in BRICS countries.

18. **Future of the BRICS** • Perspectives and future challenges for the BRICS in the new world order.

19. **Case Studies** • Detailed analysis of specific case studies related to the BRICS.

20. **Conclusion** • Final reflections on the role of the BRICS in the new world order and possible future scenarios.

1. Introduction to BRICS Definition and History of BRICS (Brazil, Russia, India, China, South Africa)

A. Definition BRICS represents an association of five major emerging economies globally: Brazil, Russia, India, China, and South Africa. The acronym "BRICS" is derived from the initials of these countries' names. Cooperation among BRICS members is centered on various areas, including economic development, politics, diplomacy, and security-related issues.

B. History • Early Years and Formation: • Initial cooperation was concentrated among four countries (Brazil, Russia, India, and China) before South Africa's inclusion in 2010. • The idea of an association among major emerging economies was first formulated in 2001 by the economist Jim O'Neill, who coined the acronym "BRIC" (prior to South Africa's inclusion).

• Development of BRICS: • Since the first meeting of finance ministers in Germany in 2006, countries recognized the importance of constructive collaboration. • The first BRICS summit meeting was held in Yekaterinburg, Russia, in 2009, marking a crucial milestone in formalizing collaboration among the countries.

• Entry of South Africa: • In 2010, South Africa was invited to join the group, and the acronym was modified from "BRIC" to "BRICS." • South Africa's inclusion introduced a new dynamic within the group and expanded its impact and scope, especially in relation to Africa and developing countries.

C. Evolution • Economic Cooperation: • BRICS has worked on promoting economic growth and sustainable development among member countries and globally. • Political and Diplomatic Platform: • In addition to economic cooperation, BRICS has provided a platform for discussing and cooperating on political and diplomatic issues. • Global Influence: • Over time, BRICS has expanded its reach, having a significant impact on global dynamics, thanks to its growing economic and political influence. • Challenges and Criticisms: • Despite being a powerful economic bloc, BRICS faces various challenges and criticisms, including internal inequalities, political divergences, and differences in goals and methodologies.

D. Objectives • Strengthening Cooperation: • The primary objective of BRICS is to strengthen cooperation among member countries and address common global issues. • Promoting Development: • BRICS aims to promote economic and social development both nationally and globally. • Equity in the Global System: • Working towards a fairer and more representative world order, challenging the existing order, and proposing new dynamics and structures.

Introduction to BRICS: In-depth Exploration and Further Aspects

Geostrategic Dimensions BRICS not only constitute an influential economic bloc but also hold a significant geostrategic position in the world. Their geographical locations and related regional spheres of influence have a substantial impact on global political and economic balances. For example, China is a key player in the Asia-Pacific, while Brazil has a prominent position in Latin America. Each member carries not only the weight of its own economy but also its regional relationships and strategic alliances.

Cultural Facets The cultural diversity among Brazil, Russia, India, China, and South Africa is remarkable and is expressed through language, religion, traditions, and social norms. This cultural plurality influences diplomacy and political decisions within the bloc, generating interesting and complex dynamics. The variety and richness of cultures represent both a challenge and an opportunity for cooperation among BRICS members.

Political Divergences Despite cohesion in some areas, significant political divergences exist among BRICS countries, manifesting in terms of domestic governance, foreign policy, and political ideologies. For instance, while India is the world's largest democracy, China is governed by a single party. These differences can affect the group's cohesion and its ability to present itself as a united entity on international issues.

Natural and Environmental Resources BRICS are endowed with abundant natural resources, including oil, natural gas, minerals, and biodiversity. The use and management of these resources are crucial both for national economies and for global ecological balance. The approach to resource management and the environment is another aspect that can both unite and divide BRICS members, given their diverse needs, priorities, and environmental challenges.

Demographic Dynamics Demographic dynamics in BRICS countries are of significant interest. For example, India and Brazil have relatively young populations, while China is experiencing demographic aging. These dynamics influence the workforce, productivity, consumer markets, and social policies, shaping the national and internal strategies of each country.

Research and Development (R&D) BRICS are actively engaged in research and development. China, in particular, has made significant investments in areas such as artificial intelligence and 5G technology. The focus on R&D can serve as a platform for collaboration within BRICS, where knowledge sharing and innovation can pave the way for shared solutions to common problems.

Collective Security The concept of collective security has gained prominence in discussions within BRICS, as they seek to navigate global security challenges while balancing national autonomy and multilateral cooperation. BRICS members collaborate on various security issues while exercising caution to preserve their sovereignty and decision-making autonomy.

Education and Skills Education and skills development are essential to support economic growth and innovation. Each BRICS country has its own challenges and goals in this sector, ranging from basic education to advanced training and 21st-century skills development.

These are just some aspects that could be further explored and developed in a detailed analysis of BRICS. Each subsection can be deepened with data, stories, and analysis to create a multidimensional understanding of BRICS, offering the reader both a panoramic and detailed view of the bloc and its dynamics. Each element could also be explored through interviews with experts, specific policy analyses, and exploration of future scenarios.

Investments and Financial Flows BRICS play an essential role in the global financial landscape. Financial flows and foreign direct investments to and from BRICS countries have become a key element in supporting global economic growth. The BRICS Bank, formally known as the New Development Bank (NDB), is a notable example of how these countries are seeking to build parallel institutions that reflect and support their development aspirations and priorities.

Legal and Regulatory Issues Legal and regulatory issues in BRICS countries are diverse and influence the business and investment environment. Differences in regulation, standards, market policies, and labor laws are relevant themes that require careful study for anyone wishing to understand the internal workings and dynamics of BRICS, both individually and as a bloc.

Labor Market Dynamics The labor market in BRICS countries represents another area deserving of detailed examination. For example, while India and Brazil are facing challenges related to a growing workforce and the need to create new job opportunities, Russia and China are navigating demographic changes and an aging working population.

Public Health The public health sector in BRICS countries is another fertile ground for research and analysis, especially in light of the challenges that emerged during the COVID-19 pandemic. The different ways in which each country has addressed the health crisis, their vaccine responses, and distribution strategies offer interesting insights into national priorities and emergency management capabilities.

Relations with Other Economic Blocs The interaction of BRICS with other economic and political blocs, such as the European Union, ASEAN, or the G7, is another aspect that can be examined to understand how these dynamics influence global geopolitics and international cooperation. This includes strategic alliances, tensions, and collaborations with other emerging economies and developed nations.

Tourism and Cultural Exchanges Tourism and cultural exchanges between BRICS countries and the rest of the world offer a rich ground for exploring how culture, art, and traditions are shared and celebrated. Each BRICS country has a unique cultural heritage and distinctive tourism landscape that can serve as a bridge to strengthen ties and promote mutual understanding.

Complex Diplomatic Relations Although BRICS as an entity share certain common goals, bilateral relations among members are characterized by complexity and diverse facets. For example, India-China relations are fraught with challenges and opportunities, existing alongside common objectives pursued through the BRICS forum.

Infrastructure and Development Projects The role of BRICS in infrastructure development—both nationally and in third-party countries, particularly through initiatives like China's Belt and Road Initiative (BRI)—is another factor that can be examined to understand how these countries are expanding their influence and promoting connectivity.

Climate Change and Sustainability The stance of BRICS on climate change and sustainability, as well as their respective national policies and international commitments on environmental issues, deserve in-depth analysis to understand the strategies and priorities of these countries in a global context.

Continuing to explore each of these aspects would provide a 360-degree view of BRICS, allowing us to delve into the internal and external dynamics that shape this influential economic and political bloc. Furthermore, examining how these themes are intertwined and influence each other will provide an even deeper insight into the challenges and opportunities emerging from interactions among Brazil, Russia, India, China, and South Africa.

Digital Economies and Cybersecurity The evolution of digital economies in BRICS countries reveals a range of dynamics that influence both internal development and external relations. While China is a giant in digital technology and e-commerce, other BRICS countries are also exploring and implementing advancements in the digital sector. In tandem, issues of cybersecurity, data protection, and privacy become crucial, especially considering the diverse stances and policies each country adopts regarding cyberspace and digitization.

Human Rights and Social Issues Issues related to human rights and social matters in BRICS nations provide another field of inquiry. Each country has specific challenges and contexts regarding civil rights, gender equality, labor rights, and social inclusion that can influence both domestic politics and international perception and relations.

Agribusiness and Food Security Agribusiness and food security represent other vital aspects to explore. Given that BRICS countries play a significant role in global food production, understanding how they manage food production, distribution, and security, not only for their citizens but also from a global market perspective, is fundamental.

Militarization and Defense Analyzing militarization programs and defense strategies of BRICS countries provides insight into power dynamics and security. Each member has its own perception of threats, defense objectives, and military alliances, contributing to a complex network of cooperation and sometimes tension within the bloc.

Migration and Mobility Migration phenomena and labor mobility between and within BRICS countries are equally significant. From India and China, known for their significant global diaspora, to Brazil and South Africa, dealing with internal and regional migration issues, exploring how people's mobility influences the economy and society becomes relevant.

Religion and National Identity Issues of religion and national identity, and how these intertwine with politics and society in each BRICS country, represent another area of analysis. The coexistence of different religions and beliefs and the role they play in shaping national and international policies, as well as inter-state relations, are themes that can be carefully explored.

Energy Policies and Resources Energy policies and the use of resources in BRICS countries, both in terms of domestic consumption and exports, offer insights into development dynamics and international trade patterns. Access to energy and the management of natural resources become focal points in international negotiations and the definition of sustainable development strategies.

Social and Economic Inequalities Social and economic inequalities within BRICS countries represent another crucial dimension. While all five countries have shown significant economic growth, there are considerable disparities in terms of wealth distribution, access to opportunities, and human development, which are reflected in various sectors of society and the economy.

Soft Power and Popular Culture Finally, soft power and the spread of popular culture from BRICS nations in the global context can be examined to understand how these countries export their culture and influence global dynamics through cinema, music, art, and other cultural expressions.

Each point mentioned above can be further developed and explored through an analytical and critical lens, seeking to understand not only current policies and practices but also how these may evolve in the future and what implications they may have at both national and international levels. Furthermore, the connection and interaction between these various themes will provide a holistic and multi-dimensional view of BRICS in the global landscape.

Conclusion of Section: Intersections and Challenges of BRICS Countries Incorporating and analyzing these different aspects around BRICS delineates an intricate framework of power, influences, challenges, and opportunities on the global stage. BRICS, while acting as a conglomerate of emerging nations with common goals and similar challenges, bring with them a series of distinct national peculiarities that often shape their interactions both within the group and globally.

The economies of BRICS, although they have shown significant development and increasing influence in recent decades, are not exempt from crucial challenges and internal contradictions. For example, while they share the ambition to reform international financial institutions and improve their status in terms of global economic governance, there are also sharp rivalries, especially in terms of regional and global leadership.

Issues related to economic and social inequalities, combined with various environmental, demographic, and human rights challenges, form a common backdrop, but they manifest in different ways in each nation. Each BRICS country has demonstrated different resilience and capacity in addressing these challenges, often drawing inspiration from or differentiating themselves from their counterparts.

For instance, China, with its massive economy and authoritarian approach to governance, presents a set of challenges and strategies that are markedly different from those of India, which, in turn, has a pluralistic democracy and a highly diverse society. Similarly, Brazil, with its internal political challenges and abundant natural resources, and Russia, with its geopolitical ambitions and energy-oriented economy, offer further contrasts and useful comparisons within the bloc.

In addition, the interaction and dialogue among the BRICS and other global actors, including both developed countries and other emerging economies, shape a mosaic of relations that oscillate between cooperation and competition. The dynamics of these relationships are often forged through a combination of factors, such as bilateral diplomacy, economic interests, strategic alliances, and global issues such as climate change and pandemic management. Each BRICS, therefore, represents a single summit in a broader network of global relations and dynamics, whose power and influence are both enhanced and limited by its respective capabilities and the complexity of internal and international challenges. Therefore, an in-depth study of the BRICS, considering both the group's common aspirations and challenges and the uniqueness of each member, can offer valuable insights into the multifaceted nature of power and influence in the contemporary world order. Exploring these points of intersection, where national challenges meet global aspirations and dynamics, provides a penetrating look into the complexities of contemporary international relations and the mechanisms through which BRICS countries pursue their interests and navigate the often tumultuous waters of global geopolitics. In summary, the collective and individual narrative of the BRICS represents a unique blend of collaboration, competition, and an ongoing quest for a more influential and recognized position within the global system. This combination of factors and dynamics contributes to defining and, at the same time, complicating the future trajectory of these key countries in the global context.

2. BRICS Economies • Analysis of each member's economy and global impact.

BRICS Economies: Analysis and Global Impact The BRICS, consisting of Brazil, Russia, India, China, and South Africa, represent a significant economic entity on the global stage. These countries, despite their cultural, political, and economic differences, have managed to create a common front, developing significant collaborations in the global economic context. Let's take a closer look at the economies of the members and the global impact of the group.

Brazil: Agriculture and Resources Brazil boasts an economy significantly powered by the agricultural sector and an abundance of natural resources. It is one of the world's major exporters of soybeans, sugar, and coffee and possesses vast reserves of iron ore and bauxite. The nation has faced notable challenges, including economic stability and social issues like inequality. Its influence within the BRICS is often delineated by its ability to provide agricultural products and raw materials.

Russia: Energy and Global Power The Russian economy is deeply rooted in its vast energy resources, particularly oil and natural gas. It is one of the largest energy exporters in the world, positioning the country as a key player in the global energy balance. Russia has often used its energy resources as a tool of foreign policy, influencing other countries and economic blocs through manipulation of energy supplies.

India: Demographics and Services India is characterized by a unique demographic and a rapidly growing services sector, with a particular strength in IT and software. With a young population and a large domestic market, India is often seen as an engine for future economic growth. However, challenges like economic inequality and geopolitical tensions with neighbors influence its economic and political trajectory.

China: Manufacturing and Global Influence China stands out as "the world's factory" with its massive manufacturing capacity and growing technological sector. The Belt and Road Initiative and other global investment strategies have solidified China's role as an influential global economic actor. Its economy, however, faces challenges such as rising debt and trade tensions with other global powers.

South Africa: Minerals and Social Challenges
South Africa, with its abundant mineral resources such as gold and diamonds, plays a critical role in the global commodities economy. However, the country faces significant social and economic challenges, including unemployment, poverty, and structural inequalities rooted in its history, which influence its economic prospects and regional stability.

Global Impact of BRICS The global implication of BRICS is undeniable. From negotiating power in international trade to foreign direct investments and influence in international financial institutions, BRICS is a bloc that cannot be overlooked. They have sought to reshape the norms and rules of the global economy, pushing for greater representation and influence in global institutions like the International Monetary Fund and the World Bank.

Conclusion Although united by common goals, the economic differences among BRICS members are significant. Understanding the internal dynamics of each country and their strategies for global interaction is crucial to deciphering the future trajectories of the bloc and the global economic system as a whole. A detailed analysis of each economy, considering the challenges and opportunities presented by each country, as well as tensions and collaborations within the group, provides an essential perspective for any discussion on the future of the global economy and international power dynamics.

The nature of the BRICS economies and their impact on the global economic order is a crucial issue for anyone seeking to understand contemporary dynamics in geopolitics and international economics. One of the most intriguing aspects of BRICS is the diversity of their economies and how this diversity is both a source of strength and a potential point of friction within the group.

The BRICS economies are distinctly different yet integrative. While Brazil and South Africa are agricultural and mineral powers, Russia is an energy superpower. At the same time, India has an economy dominated by the services sector, particularly IT and related services, while China is a global manufacturing powerhouse. This combination of economic skills and focuses potentially allows BRICS to act as a comprehensive economic bloc, capable of self-sufficiency to some extent while being well-integrated into the global economy.

However, it is essential to note that there are significant economic and developmental disparities among BRICS members. While China has experienced incredible economic growth and is now one of the world's largest economies, other countries like Brazil and South Africa have faced significant challenges in terms of economic growth and sustainable development. Additionally, while India has one of the youngest populations in the world, which could potentially translate into a demographic dividend, Russia is facing an aging population, which could have significant implications for its future economic growth and the sustainability of its welfare model.

The issue of international disparities within BRICS is also relevant when considering the distribution of wealth within these countries. For example, despite its impressive economic growth, China faces significant challenges in terms of income inequality and wealth distribution. Similarly, India has one of the most unequal wealth distributions in the world, with a significant portion of its population still living in extreme poverty.

These internal factors, combined with external challenges and the global economic environment, are critical to understanding the trajectory and future prospects of BRICS economies. For example, trade tensions between China and the United States not only have direct implications for the Chinese economy but, given the interconnected nature of global economies, have ripple effects that influence all BRICS members and beyond.

In terms of global economic governance, BRICS have sought to challenge and reform existing economic institutions, promoting greater inclusivity and representation for developing countries. The creation of the BRICS New Development Bank is an example of such an effort, aimed at providing an alternative to Bretton Woods institutions and promoting development and financing models more aligned with the needs and priorities of developing countries.

Each BRICS member, with its unique economic challenges and specific global aspirations, brings to the table a set of expectations and goals that they seek to navigate through intra-BRICS cooperation and interactions with the global economy. The interplay between competitiveness and cooperation, both within the bloc and between BRICS and other key economic actors, will significantly shape the future global economic landscape.

In a scenario where multilateralism is under strain, and protectionism is gaining ground in various parts of the world, BRICS represent an interesting amalgamation of South-South cooperation and the rise of emerging countries seeking a seat at the global economic decision-making table. Their ability to negotiate as a bloc and propose alternatives to the existing global economic system will be crucial in understanding and anticipating the future dynamics of the world economy.

In the intricate web of the BRICS economies, observing the methodologies adopted for managing economic challenges and channeling opportunities becomes an essential journey through various economic strategies and models. The intertwining of monetary, fiscal, and trade policies, along with specific growth and development trajectories, provides a mosaic of examples of how emerging states are adapting and responding to the pressures and challenges of the global economic environment.

While BRICS members have built a certain degree of solidarity as a group, they also exhibit various forms of economic rivalry and contrasts. For example, competition between India and China in various sectors, including technology and entry into global markets, has created a dynamic that is both cooperative and competitive. Political and military tensions, particularly along their common borders, have further complicated the economic relationship, influencing bilateral trade and foreign direct investments.

Similarly, Brazil and China, despite being significant trading partners, are also competitors in certain export markets, such as those in Latin America and Africa, where both seek to expand their economic and political influence. The nature of these interactions exemplifies how economic alliances like BRICS can simultaneously accommodate elements of cooperation and competition among their members.

Debt issues are another fundamental aspect in the exploration of the BRICS economies. While some members like China have accumulated significant foreign currency reserves, others like Brazil have faced challenges related to foreign debt and import dependence. South Africa, in turn, has grappled with issues related to public debt and stagnant growth, further complicated by the economic impact of the COVID-19 pandemic.

The BRICS' relationship with nations outside the bloc is another vital strand of discussion. While they seek to coordinate their economic policies and projects, the BRICS also actively interact with non-BRICS nations, both bilaterally and through multilateral forums. The approach taken by the BRICS toward economically powerful nations like the United States, the European Union, and Japan, as well as toward other developing countries in Asia, Africa, and Latin America, has a significant influence on global trade flows, investment patterns, and the dynamics of economic geopolitics.

The way BRICS position themselves within global value chains is another relevant dimension for understanding their economies. China, for example, is deeply integrated into global value chains, becoming a nodal point for the production and export of manufactured goods. India, on the other hand, has sought to increase its participation in global value chains, particularly in the services sector, but has been hindered by various challenges, including the need for reforms in manufacturing and infrastructure.

The ongoing dialogue on climate change and sustainability also has significant implications for the BRICS economies, which have been forced to balance the need for economic growth with global pressure to adopt more sustainable practices and reduce carbon emissions. The transition to a green economy represents an additional challenge, given the dependence of some BRICS members on natural resource exports and energy-intensive production.

The multidimensionality of the BRICS economies, with their various facets of collaboration and competition, not only within the bloc but also in a broader global context, reflects the complexity of their economic interactions and their impact on the global economic architecture. Future scenarios will depend on how these countries navigate their internal divergences, while simultaneously building a united front in global economic negotiations, and how they react and adapt to the evolving dynamics and challenges of the world economy.

The economies of the BRICS, although imbued with dynamism and resilience, are not immune to vulnerabilities, which manifest in various ways and across various sectors. Considering the realm of currencies, their stability and strength in global financial markets have been subjects of analysis and discussion. The Indian Rupee and the South African Rand, for example, have shown significant volatility against the US dollar and other strong currencies, while the Russian Ruble has experienced periods of instability due in part to geopolitical factors and energy price fluctuations.

Additionally, the technology sector, representing a vital and growing part of the global economy, brings various challenges and opportunities for BRICS nations. While China has reached advanced levels in the technology sector, with companies like Alibaba and Tencent holding significant global presence, India has shown explosive growth in its startup ecosystem, creating innovations and solutions in digital technology, fintech, and more. Russia has solidified its presence in the cybersecurity and information technology sectors, while Brazil and South Africa are seeking to enhance their own technology sectors through investments and partnerships.

Another dimension deserving deep reflection is that of economic and environmental sustainability. While these nations seek to expand their economic growth, the pressure to do so in an environmentally sustainable and socially responsible manner is increasing. China, for example, faces the challenge of balancing its rapid industrialization with the need to reduce emissions and minimize environmental impact. Additionally, the issue of sustainability also encompasses social challenges such as equity, inclusion, and social justice, elements that are essential for ensuring growth that benefits the entire society.

Investment flows among BRICS nations and beyond the bloc represent another crucial aspect. Each of these countries is actively seeking to attract foreign direct investment (FDI) to catalyze development and economic growth while also expanding their investment horizons globally. China's Belt and Road Initiative is an emblematic example of how a BRICS nation is seeking to shape global economic dynamics through large-scale infrastructure investments.

In terms of domestic politics, each of the BRICS economies faces distinct challenges related to demography, governance, and social stability. India, with its incredibly young demographic, faces pressure to create job opportunities and support economic growth that can absorb the enormous cohort of young people entering the labor market each year. Brazil, on the other hand, must address issues related to social and economic inequality, while Russia is confronted with challenges posed by an aging population and the need to diversify its economy.

The issue of human rights and civil liberties, democratic governance, and the rule of law is also intertwined with economic discourse. How each BRICS country addresses these issues influences global perception, foreign investments, and bilateral and multilateral relations. Being able to navigate the challenges of internal governance while pursuing economic growth and maintaining a position of strength and cooperation on the global stage is a crucial and complex dynamic within the economic strategies of the BRICS.

In any case, the influence of the BRICS and their impact on the world go beyond mere economic dominance, infiltrating political, cultural, and social spheres on a global level. Understanding these diverse, complex, and interconnected spheres requires in-depth analysis that integrates various sectors and disciplines, examining both internal and external dynamics to provide a holistic framework of their trajectories and future implications.

In the landscape of the BRICS economies, the balance between maintaining economic growth and managing inequality emerges as a crucial friction point. These nations have experienced significant economic expansions; however, in many cases, this has not necessarily led to an equitable distribution of wealth. For example, in countries like Brazil and South Africa, where economic inequality is particularly pronounced, the gap between the wealthiest and poorest sectors of society remains a significant political and social issue. The equitable distribution of resources, educational opportunities, and access to vital infrastructure are all issues that impact the sustainability of economic growth and development.

On the other hand, there is the issue of integrating the BRICS economies into the context of the global economy, not only in terms of trade but also concerning global networks of production and distribution. For example, the global health crisis has revealed both the resilience and vulnerabilities of global supply chains, highlighting dependence on certain countries (such as China) for key products and materials, as well as the vulnerabilities associated with this type of interdependence. Balancing the promotion of national self-sufficiency with encouraging global economic integration remains a delicate issue for the BRICS economies.

Furthermore, as the BRICS seek to increase their weight and influence in the world economy, they will also need to navigate the sometimes tumultuous waters of international relations and geopolitics. Tensions between member countries, such as those between India and China, as well as tensions with other global economic entities, will inevitably shape the path that the BRICS take in the future. Managing these tensions and maintaining constructive bilateral and multilateral relationships will be essential for their collective and individual success on the global stage.

Energy represents another fundamental sector within the analysis of the BRICS economies. As the world gradually shifts toward cleaner and more sustainable energy sources, the BRICS, together representing a significant portion of global energy consumption, have a crucial role to play in this transition. China and India, in particular, due to their enormous populations and expanding industries, have a significant impact on global energy consumption patterns. Their ability to implement renewable energy technologies and promote sustainable practices within their borders will have a substantial influence on the effectiveness of global efforts to combat climate change.

The theme of innovation and technological adoption runs through all sectors of the BRICS economies. The ability to generate, adopt, and disseminate new technologies not only drives economic growth but also facilitates the solution of social, economic, and environmental problems. Innovation is not limited to digital technology but extends to all sectors, including agriculture, where the adoption of sustainable and innovative agricultural practices can have a significant impact on food security, resource management, and the environment.

Education and skill development represent another crucial pillar within the mosaic of the BRICS economies. These nations' ability to develop talents and skills that meet the needs of their evolving economies, and to do so equitably and accessibly, will significantly impact their ability to sustain long-term economic growth and stability. Education not only fuels innovation and economic growth but also contributes to promoting informed and engaged citizenship, essential for stable governance and social development.

Thus, while navigating the vast network of challenges and opportunities presented by the BRICS economies, it is crucial to recognize the interconnectedness of various sectors and issues and how decisions and policies in one area inevitably influence others. This interdependence underscores the importance of a holistic and integrated approach to understanding and guiding the future development of the BRICS within the global context.

In conclusion, the economic profile of the BRICS stands out as a rich and complex landscape, where growth trajectories, inherent challenges, and future prospects of the five emerging economies interact in a system of mutual influences and dependencies with the global economic environment.

The heterogeneity of their economies, with China emerging as a global economic superpower, India showcasing substantial growth potential, Russia balancing its economy between challenges and opportunities, Brazil navigating the complexity of its internal disparities, and South Africa seeking a sustainable development path, represents an economic mosaic in which each of these states assumes different but integrated roles within the context of the BRICS.

The diversification of their economic foundations, the balance between industry and agriculture, the services sector, and the ability to manage and implement technological innovations are fundamental elements that determine the direction of their economies. Navigating the need to ensure growth and development while maintaining a balance with environmental protection, social sustainability, and natural resource management presents significant challenges but also offers insights into alternative economic development models.

Similarly, the issue of socio-economic inequalities, both domestically and in the context of international relations, emerges as a predominant concern. The BRICS' ability to address internal inequalities by promoting broader economic and social inclusion and to establish international relations that do not further exacerbate existing disparities will be crucial for their future path and the evolution of their global role.

Furthermore, the interplay of politics and economics in BRICS dynamics underscores how the economic paths pursued by these countries are intrinsically linked to their geopolitical strategies, internal dynamics, and global ambitions. Political tensions, both internally and among BRICS countries, could serve as catalysts or inhibitors of joint economic cooperation processes, thus influencing the form and substance of joint economic initiatives and the stability of the BRICS coalition itself.

Finally, the BRICS, with their growing economic weight and influence on the world stage, are called upon to navigate a transforming global economic order, reconciling their own aspirations with the responsibilities that emerge from their increasing influence. The ability to balance national interests with those of the global collective, and to do so in a way that not only ensures economic growth and development but also promotes sustainability, equity, and stability, will be essential in shaping not only the future of the BRICS but also the global economy as a whole.

The analysis of the BRICS economies, therefore, must be conducted with a perspective that transcends individual economic metrics and incorporates a holistic and integrated assessment of the multiple factors, dynamics, and challenges that will shape their future and the role they will play in defining the global economic order in the decades to come.

3. BRICS Policies Examination of the internal and external policies of BRICS countries.

The politics of BRICS, composed of Brazil, Russia, India, China, and South Africa, encompasses a wide range of issues and challenges, as these states exhibit significant diversity in their political structures, policy priorities, and ideological orientations. Examining both the internal and external policies of these nations can shed light on how they mutually influence one another and shape the global geopolitical and geo-economic context.

Internal Policies

Brazil Brazil, with its democratic system and emerging economy, has navigated various internal issues, including political corruption, social tensions, and challenges related to the sustainability of economic development and social justice. The fight against poverty and inequality, along with the management of natural resources and biodiversity, represents central political issues.

Russia Russia, guided by a centralized power model, faces dilemmas associated with managing internal ethnic and religious diversity, an economy based on energy resources, and tensions with the West. Issues related to civil liberties, democracy, and the role of independent institutions are also relevant.

India India, the world's largest democracy, confronts challenges related to religious and ethnic pluralism, social and economic inequalities, and its rapid development. Balancing economic growth, environmental protection, and social inclusion represents a critical knot.

China China, under the Communist Party, navigates the management of economic growth, social stability, and the assertion of its governance model. Issues such as human rights, freedom of expression, and the management of technological innovation are relevant aspects.

South Africa South Africa, with its history of apartheid and current challenges related to economic inequality, corruption, and the management of social tensions, pursues a political path focused on reconciliation, economic renewal, and social justice.

External Policies

Cooperation and Competition BRICS work together in some areas, such as finance and development, but also exhibit competition, especially in terms of global influence and access to resources.

Global Governance BRICS actively seek to redefine and reform global governance institutions, aiming for greater weight and representation for emerging economies.

Global Security Relations between BRICS countries and other global actors are crucial in managing issues such as terrorism, nuclear proliferation, and regional conflicts.

Environment and Sustainable Development Joint commitment to addressing climate change and promoting sustainable development while maintaining their economic growth agendas is a key area of foreign policy.

Trade and Investments While striving to develop their domestic markets, BRICS also actively engage in creating global trade and investment opportunities, sometimes through bilateral and multilateral agreements.

The convergence of BRICS' internal and external policies generates an ongoing dialogue between the need to address domestic issues and the ambition to forge an influential role on the international stage. Each country brings its own strengths, challenges, and expectations to the BRICS cooperation table, seeking to chart a path that safeguards not only national interests but also promotes a more inclusive and equitable world order. Exploring the political dynamics within and among the BRICS, therefore, offers a window through which to observe the tensions, alliances, and aspirations shaping the contemporary world.

Each BRICS country presents a unique political matrix, revealing a blend of convergences and divergences that stimulate both collaboration and contrast on the international stage. The fluidity of their internal and external policies represents a fascinating dynamic between individual national interests and the collective interest of the BRICS coalition.

As we further explore the foreign policies of BRICS countries, it becomes evident that while these countries seek to promote a more multipolar world order, each of their approaches is deeply rooted in their own national challenges and aspirations. For example, China has adopted the "One Belt, One Road" (OBOR) initiative to extend its economic-political influence through an extensive network of countries. On the other hand, India has maintained a cautious balance between its commitment to BRICS and its growing ties with Western democracies, particularly through the Quad, a strategic dialogue forum that also involves the United States, Japan, and Australia.

Regarding **internal politics**, issues such as democracy, human rights, and governance become even more crucial. Let's take Brazil, for example: its internal political dynamics have been characterized by significant polarizations, with direct implications for its foreign policy and interactions within BRICS. Similarly, in South Africa, the dominant theme of ongoing struggle against economic and social inequality, which strongly resonates in its foreign policy, seeks to create South-South alliances and promote a more equitable international order.

Furthermore, BRICS have made efforts to coordinate their policies in various international forums, including those related to trade, climate, and security. Despite their divergences, as seen in contrasts regarding issues such as the reform of international financial institutions or support for specific regimes or movements, there has been a certain coherence in their collective commitment to challenge the Western-dominated world order.

The issue of human rights and democracy, often addressed disparately by BRICS countries, underscores the diverse governance philosophies and political values that exist within the group. While some countries strongly emphasize sovereignty and non-interference, others explore ways to reconcile respect for universal human rights with the desire to maintain stable bilateral relations.

In terms of trade and the economy, BRICS seek to articulate a shared vision of sustainable development and inclusive growth while navigating rivalry and competition, both within the group and with external actors. For example, trade tensions between India and China or competition in the energy sector between Russia and Brazil provide a framework for understanding the complexities and inherent challenges in managing relations among countries with global and regional ambitions.

In the context of global security and peace, BRICS have demonstrated a combination of cooperation and disagreement. For example, while there has been a degree of consistency in supporting the principle of non-interference in the internal affairs of states, BRICS have shown divergences on issues such as the crisis in Syria or the Iranian nuclear issue, reflecting the various security concerns and strategic objectives of individual members.

As a coalition, BRICS continue to explore pathways to deeper integration and the promotion of their common goals on the global stage, despite tensions and challenges arising from their unique political realities and divergences in values and national interests. Their future trajectory will continue to oscillate between cooperation and competition, offering a fascinating and complex view of global geopolitics.

Within the fabric of BRICS policies, themes of social justice, innovation, and sustainability emerge as common threads capturing attention at both national and international levels. Delving deeper into this intricate fabric, we can discover further nuances that reflect how these nations address emerging challenges and opportunities in the contemporary world order.

For example, the impact of digitization and new technologies is evident throughout the entire coalition. China has vigorously pushed for leadership in the technology sector, exploring the realm of digital currency and seeking to establish new standards for the internet of the future. On the other hand, India has used digital innovation to address national challenges such as financial inclusion and access to healthcare services, while balancing innovation with issues related to privacy and data security.

The way in which BRICS navigate the waters of globalization and economic nationalism represents another intriguing aspect. While Brazil, for example, has a history of oscillating between open policies and more protectionist strategies, Russia has balanced its desire to attract foreign investments with the need to protect its key sectors. Meanwhile, South Africa has sought to balance the need for foreign investment with the imperative of promoting local development and black economic empowerment.

Climate challenges represent another prism through which to explore BRICS policies. The global imperative to address climate change sees these nations balancing the need for economic growth with the pressure to adopt sustainable measures. For instance, while China has announced ambitious plans to achieve carbon neutrality by 2060, it must still balance this goal with its short-term reliance on coal. India, on the other hand, is striving to leverage its abundance of sunlight to become a leader in solar energy, although it must grapple with challenges related to energy access and security.

Additionally, the theme of global governance and the role of BRICS in shaping international institutions provide a novel view of their policy. The desire to reform institutions such as the International Monetary Fund and the World Bank, as well as the United Nations, reflects BRICS' aspiration to shape a world order that better represents their interests and those of other developing countries. The establishment of the BRICS New Development Bank represents a step in this direction, although it remains to be seen how this and other similar initiatives will develop in the future.

The interaction between the BRICS and other nations and blocs, such as the European Union and the United States, adds another layer to their political practice. While their interaction with these actors has encompassed both collaboration and competition, the dynamics underscore the BRICS' desire to be recognized as key players on the world stage, capable of shaping and influencing global dynamics in significant ways.

In the context of security, the BRICS have addressed a range of issues, including challenges related to terrorism, maritime piracy, and cybersecurity, seeking to coordinate responses while navigating their divergences. The management of the terrorism threat, in particular, has seen the need to balance security concerns with human rights and social justice.

Therefore, the policies of the BRICS are immersed in a rich and multifaceted landscape, woven together by threads of cooperation, competition, and conflict. Exploring the various facets of these policies not only provides insight into their internal dynamics but also offers valuable insights into their aspirations, concerns, and strategies in the broader global context.

Analyzing the projection of the BRICS on the global stage is further enriched by considering the theme of soft power and the realm of cultural and societal relations between these countries and the rest of the world. The promotion of culture, values, and national symbols, and how they influence international relations between the BRICS and other countries, becomes a significant area of exploration.

For example, China, with its ambitious "Belt and Road Initiative," seeks not only to expand its economic influence but also to increase its soft power in Asia,

Africa, and Europe, using tools such as infrastructure investments, trade, as well as cultural and educational exchanges. India, through its "Act East" policy and support for the global Indian diaspora, actively engages in forging ties based not only on economic or strategic interests but also on cultural and social ones.

Furthermore, the dynamics of intra-BRICS relations offer a window through which to explore how these nations manage their differences and leverage areas of convergence. For instance, while China and India have various unresolved issues, including border disputes, they seek areas of cooperation in multilateral forums, including the BRICS platform. This coexistence of contrasts and collaboration is a recurring theme within the BRICS, which experience frequent friction, such as in taxation and trade matters, but find common ground on issues like reforming international financial institutions or addressing climate change.

The concept of leadership within the BRICS is also of particular interest. The way each country perceives its own role and contribution within the group and towards the outside world varies significantly. While China may see itself as the natural leader of the BRICS due to its economic size and global weight, India, Brazil, Russia, and South Africa also bring their own aspirations and visions of regional and global leadership to the table, sometimes conflicting with the Chinese agenda.

In the context of global politics and security, the BRICS seek to outline a joint narrative, even though their specific actions and positions may diverge. Their common opposition to what they perceive as a unilateral world order dominated by the United States unites them, but their specific geopolitical and geoeconomic interests can also divide them, as seen in their approaches to global and regional crises.

The influence of the BRICS in resolving or mitigating regional conflicts represents another crucial aspect to explore. For example, considering Russia's role in Syria or China's stance on North Korea, we see nations trying to balance their strategic interests with the need to project a sense of responsibility and global leadership. Similarly, the approach of India and South Africa to peace and security issues in their neighborhoods reflects a combination of security concerns, economic interests, and a desire to project influence and leadership.

Finally, the question of what future awaits the BRICS in an evolving world characterized by growing challenges, such as superpower rivalry, global crises, and systemic change, offers further insights into how the internal and external policies of these nations will evolve in the near future. Will they be able to overcome their differences and forge a more cohesive and influential coalition? Or will internal divergences and external challenges limit their impact and coherence on the global stage? Navigating through these questions provides an intriguing journey through the complexities and contradictions of the BRICS in the contemporary world.

Another interesting dimension in the analysis of BRICS policies concerns the management of inequality and social cohesion within these countries. Despite achieving significant economic milestones in recent decades, BRICS nations continue to grapple with acute economic disparities, corruption issues, and human rights challenges.

The issue of inequality manifests through various prisms. In Brazil, for example, economic and social disparities are closely intertwined with issues of race and gender, and the nation regularly faces tensions related to these socioeconomic differentiations. In South Africa, the shadows of apartheid continue to reflect in economic disparities and social tension, with persistent issues related to access to economic opportunities and essential services among different communities.

Russia presents a distinct political landscape in which the centralization of power and nationalism play a key role in shaping its political strategy, both domestically and internationally. Economic and social imbalances are often obscured by a robust patriotic narrative and skillful media management. There is an ongoing dialogue about the role of NGOs and the space for civil society in a country that balances the demand for order and stability with the need for innovation and development.

In the Indian context, pluralism, both cultural and religious, continues to be a defining feature but also a challenge for its politics. Managing diversity and promoting social cohesion are central themes, given the various tensions arising from economic inequalities, religious differences, and regional disparities. Promoting a cohesive national identity while managing this plurality is a constant political challenge.

China's approach to politics, with its centralized government model and strong control by the Communist Party, presents another facet of the BRICS. Emphasis on social harmony and stability, combined with strong economic leadership, has defined China's success. However, issues such as tensions in regions like Tibet and Xinjiang, as well as the treatment of ethnic and religious minorities, highlight the challenges of managing diversity within such a political model.

It is also crucial to consider the evolution of the BRICS in the digital era, as technology becomes an increasingly critical field in determining global power and influence. Each BRICS country is navigating its own challenges and opportunities in this realm. For example, while India and China have made significant strides in the tech sector, becoming leaders in specific segments such as e-commerce and mobile technologies, they face challenges such as regulating the tech industry, data privacy and cybersecurity issues, and bridging the digital divide domestically.

An in-depth analysis of the BRICS takes us through a kaleidoscope of political challenges and strategies, navigating the desire for internal stability, economic growth, and an influential presence on the world stage. Each nation, while sharing certain common aspirations, pursues its unique goals through a variety of methods and policies, often creating a set of practices that are as harmonious as they are contrasting. Future challenges, including global changes, new power dynamics, and internal challenges, will provide further facets and directions to the political actions of the BRICS, continually offering new terrain and scenarios for analysis and understanding of these emerging powers.

In summary, despite considerable differences in terms of political structure, governance, and approaches to global issues, the BRICS have been able to maintain a united front in various strategic areas, primarily related to the economy and development. Their cooperation, highlighted through a series of summits and joint initiatives, reflects a mutual understanding of the importance of shaping a world order that represents their aspirations and interests.

The domestic politics of each BRICS country reflects a complex tapestry of development aspirations, the pursuit of stability, and the management of diverse socioeconomic and cultural challenges. Political stability is often balanced with pressing issues such as inequality, corruption, and the pressure for democratization in some nations. Each BRICS state, with its nuances and contexts, seeks to navigate these challenges by shaping policies that can reflect both internal aspirations and those of the coalition.

Externally, the BRICS seek to position themselves as key players in a world order undergoing significant transformations. The rise of China as a global superpower, the increasing influence of India in South Asia, Russia's role in European and Middle Eastern security issues, and the engagement of Brazil and South Africa in their respective regions are all examples of how these nations are trying to shape global and regional dynamics.

However, the future path of the BRICS is not without uncertainties and challenges. The strength of cooperation among members, the ability to navigate growing rivalries (such as between China and India), and their effectiveness in balancing aspirations, conflicts, and cooperation will be key factors in determining the bloc's role and impact on the global stage in the coming years.

Therefore, observing the BRICS through the prism of domestic and foreign politics not only provides insights into how these nations are navigating an era of significant global changes but also how they are trying to define and shape these changes according to their own visions and interests. A future is envisaged in which the BRICS bloc will continue to play a key role, traversing and influencing the many facets of the dynamic international chessboard.

4. International Relations • Analysis of Relations between BRICS and Other Global Actors

International Relations and BRICS

When examining BRICS' international relations, it is crucial to observe not only the interactions among group members but also how the bloc and individual nations relate to other global and regional actors.

1. Intra-BRICS Relations: • Despite various challenges and tensions (such as territorial disputes between India and China), BRICS have maintained a relatively united front in various international forums, highlighting cooperation in the economic and sustainable development sectors. • The BRICS platform has been used to explore and establish alternative financial mechanisms, such as the New Development Bank, aimed at providing financial resources for infrastructure and sustainable development projects among member countries and other emerging economies.

2. Relations with G7 and the West: • BRICS often position themselves as an alternative voice to that of more industrialized countries represented by the G7. • BRICS countries frequently seek to balance their relationship with Western nations, attempting to create spaces for economic cooperation while expressing disagreements on issues such as global trade norms and international governance.

3. Regional Influence: • Countries like Brazil and South Africa play significant roles in their respective regions (Latin America and Sub-Saharan Africa, respectively) and often act as bridges between BRICS and their regions. • Russia and China, with their considerable political and military influence, have developed networks of alliances and cooperation not only with each other but also with countries in the Middle East, Central Asia, and South Asia.

4. Relations with Developing Countries: • BRICS often present themselves as representatives of the interests of developing countries, emphasizing themes like global economic justice, debt, and trade. • In many instances, these nations have sought to provide development assistance and economic support to other emerging economies, cultivating alliances and supporting issues of common interest in international forums.

5. Competition and Collaboration: • While maintaining a degree of cohesion as a bloc, BRICS countries also compete with each other in various areas, such as attracting foreign investments, dominating specific global markets, and leading in global issues. • In terms of security, there are both contrasts and confluences of interests, as evidenced by Sino-Indian and Russo-Chinese relations, navigating between strategic alliances and regional tensions.

6. Global Issues and Governance: • BRICS have sought to exert influence on global governance issues, such as climate change, international security, and global health. • The role of BRICS in future dynamics of global climate politics, particularly considering the growing pressure for ambitious climate action, will be crucial, as countries like China and India are among the largest greenhouse gas emitters.

In conclusion, BRICS navigate a complex web of international relations, managing internal tensions while seeking to cultivate collective and individual influence on a global scale. The coherence and effectiveness of their foreign policies, as well as how they balance national interests with global and regional commitments, will be vital in shaping the future dynamics of the global geopolitical landscape. Examining how various BRICS countries manage these balances and their ambitions is crucial for understanding the future trajectories of the world order.

Further examining the international relations between BRICS nations and other global actors, it is crucial to delineate how diplomatic, economic, and strategic relationships have developed and how these may shape future events on the international stage.

7. Trade and Investments: • BRICS represent a powerful entity in global trade, actively participating in global value chains and emerging markets. Cooperation and competition within and outside the bloc offer opportunities and challenges in terms of market access, protectionism, and reform of international financial institutions. • China's Belt and Road Initiative is a paradigmatic example of how BRICS nations are extending their global economic influence, simultaneously creating opportunities and tensions within the bloc and with other international actors.

8. Technology and Innovation: • The race for technological leadership between BRICS and other global actors underscores the increasing role of technology and innovation in determining global power dynamics. • BRICS, particularly China and India, have become significant sources of technological innovation and are seeking to establish norms and standards in the digital and technological space globally, often challenging Western approaches and dominance.

9. Global and Regional Security: • Regional tensions, such as those in the Himalayas between China and India and security challenges faced by Russia in Europe, demonstrate how security issues can have implications both bilaterally within the BRICS bloc and globally. • The management and mediation of conflicts and how BRICS position themselves on global security and peace issues are vital aspects of their impact and influence in the world order.

10. Global Governance: • Participation and influence in global governance institutions, such as the United Nations, the International Monetary Fund, and the World Bank, remain crucial focal points of BRICS' foreign policy strategy. • Promoting a multipolar world order has been a constant theme in BRICS joint declarations, implying a direct challenge to traditional Western dominance in many international institutions and practices.

11. Environment and Sustainability: • Challenges related to climate change, biodiversity, and environmental sustainability are central to international agendas, and the BRICS play a significant role, being both major emitters and key nations for biodiversity conservation. • Global environmental governance, trade-offs between development and sustainability, and inherent tensions regarding equity in the context of climate action and environmental protection emerge as key themes in BRICS' external relations.

12. Sustainable Development: • BRICS nations, with their considerable demographic and economic weight, have a significant impact on global progress towards the United Nations Sustainable Development Goals. • BRICS' sustainable development policies and their role in South-South development represent an essential aspect of their international relations as they seek to shape the global development agenda in ways that reflect their interests and priorities.

13. Cultural Diplomacy and People-to-People: • Cultural diplomacy and "people-to-people" connections represent a crucial element in strengthening intra-BRICS cohesion and enhancing the bloc's perception and influence on a global scale. • Initiatives such as academic forums, cultural exchanges, and youth exchanges are vital tools for building bridges and promoting mutual understanding among BRICS societies and beyond.

As the BRICS pursue their path to assert and consolidate their influence on the international stage, managing these multiple and complex dynamics of external relations will be crucial. How the BRICS navigate through these various spheres and how they balance cooperation and competition, convergence and divergence, within the bloc and in their global relations, will remain central in shaping future geopolitical and geoeconomic trajectories.

Exploring the international relations of BRICS nations further delves into geopolitical and diplomatic dynamics.

14. Power Dynamics and Competition: • Competition between BRICS and Western powers, especially with the United States and the European Union, shapes a new geography of global power. The increasing influence of BRICS on the world stage is often perceived as a challenge to the Western-led liberal order. • Growing strategic rivalry, for example, in the context of 5G technology, where China emerges as a global leader, impacts global security and international alliances, with implications for digital sovereignty and cybersecurity.

15. Multilateral Diplomacy: • BRICS' engagement in multilateral platforms such as the G20, the World Trade Organization, and various UN agencies illustrates their aspiration to shape international norms and agreements. • BRICS' ability to work cohesively and present united fronts or coordinated positions in multilateral forums has the potential to strengthen their collective influence in the architecture of global governance.

16. Defense and Military Strategies: • The arms and military capabilities of BRICS, especially Russia and China, are essential themes in their projection of global power and in their relations with other nations. • Defense cooperation, through joint military exercises and security dialogues, strengthens intra-BRICS ties and helps coordinate positions on regional and global security issues.

17. Human Rights and Democracy: • The issue of human rights and the promotion of democracy play a role in the external relations of BRICS, as their perspective often contrasts with the Western approach. • Tensions related to human rights and democratic governance, as evidenced by international criticism and sanctions, represent a crucial dimension in BRICS' international relations, influencing their global image and soft power.

18. Epidemics and Global Health: • The COVID-19 pandemic has underscored the importance of international cooperation and coordination in global health, highlighting both synergies and tensions between BRICS and other global actors. • Access to vaccines, responses to global health emergencies, and cooperation in public health fall within the broader context of BRICS' international relations, influencing perceptions of their leadership and solidarity on a global level.

19. Energy and Natural Resources: • Energy security and access to natural resources are key issues, with BRICS playing a fundamental role in global energy markets and resource-related dynamics. • Energy security strategies, investments in renewable energy, and policies related to climate change are factors that influence bilateral and multilateral relations among BRICS and with other global actors.

20. Migration and Refugees: • Migration flows and refugee crises pose both a challenge and an opportunity for BRICS nations, both domestically and in their external relations. • Migration policies, the integration of migrants and refugees, and international collaboration on migration issues have implications for social stability, economic growth, and international cooperation among the BRICS and beyond.

Managing and navigating through these key areas and the ongoing evolution of international relations between BRICS nations and other global actors offer a complex and multidimensional overview. The impact of these factors and their interconnection creates a mosaic of cooperation and conflict, synergies and tensions that the BRICS must balance to maintain and build their influence and leadership globally.

21. Technology and Cybersecurity: • BRICS nations play a central role in global technological development and cybersecurity, exploring various scenarios of cooperation and competition. China, for instance, has been at the forefront of implementing 5G technologies, while India has made significant strides in IT and software services. • Cybersecurity issues, such as cyberattacks, cyber espionage, and data protection, influence not only intra-BRICS relations but also dynamics with other global actors, posing new challenges in digital diplomacy and global security.

22. Investments and Trade: • Trade relations between BRICS nations and the rest of the world are complex and multifaceted. While significant investment flows and trade occur within the bloc, trade tensions, such as those between China and the United States, shape a competitive global environment. •

China's Belt and Road Initiative, investment initiatives in Africa, and regional integration in Latin America and Asia are examples of the depth and complexity of trade and investment dynamics that characterize the BRICS in the global context.

23. Environment and Climate Change: • The environmental policies and responses to climate change of BRICS nations have significant global impact due to their size and economic weight. China and India, in particular, are among the largest greenhouse gas emitters, and their energy and environmental policies are under international scrutiny. • BRICS' participation in international climate agreements, such as the Paris Agreement, and their national strategies for energy transition and biodiversity protection constitute an important dimension of their external relations and global impact.

24. Terrorism and Security: • The threat of terrorism and violent extremism intersects with the international relations of BRICS. Cooperation on counterterrorism, intelligence information sharing, and coordination in international forums are essential for addressing transnational security threats. • From insurgencies in various African regions to tensions in Kashmir and Chechen issues in Russia, the issue of terrorism has both national and international implications for BRICS, influencing their diplomacy and security policies.

25. Scientific Cooperation and Research: • Cooperation in scientific and research fields among BRICS and with other international partners is essential for technological advancement and sustainable development. Collaboration in space missions, medical research, and AI opens new horizons of partnership and competition. • Scientific diplomacy and academic exchanges represent another layer of BRICS' international relations, where sharing and competing for know-how, innovations, and scientific discoveries shape interactions and influence global dynamics.

26. Culture and Soft Power: • Promoting culture and exercising soft power through media, art, sports, and education are key strategies used by BRICS to build their own image and influence globally. For example, the spread of Chinese culture through Confucius Institutes worldwide. • Cultural diplomacy and the promotion of tourism among BRICS nations and beyond contribute to building bridges and influencing mutual perceptions, thereby impacting human exchanges and international relations.

The international relations of BRICS are woven through a complex network of collaboration and competition in various areas, including but not limited to those listed. The interaction between these factors and their impact on global dynamics provides fertile ground for further analysis and discussion, exploring how the BRICS shape and are shaped by the contemporary international context.

27. Multilateral Diplomacy: • BRICS play a decisive role in numerous multilateral forums, such as the UN, G20, and WTO, influencing global regulations and governance. The BRICS' approach to multilateral diplomacy often alternates between collaboration and contention, depending on the issues and interests at stake. • Their ability to shape the global order is intricate and varied, given the diversity of member countries and their respective international agendas, with India, for example, advocating for UN Security Council reform, and China strengthening its role in the WTO.

28. Energy and Resources: • BRICS are significant actors in the global energy landscape, with Russia being one of the largest exporters of natural gas and oil, and China being one of the largest consumers. Energy market dynamics, pipeline routes, and energy policies are all integral parts of their external relations. • Investments in renewable energy, such as solar energy in India and wind projects in Brazil, along with the need to ensure access to key resources like rare earth metals, are all aspects that permeate BRICS' foreign policy and influence relations with other countries and regional blocs.

29. Globalization vs. Nationalism: • Striking a balance between globalization trends and nationalist impulses is another key element in BRICS' foreign policy. For example, while China often promotes a narrative of globalization, within the context of economic nationalism, Russia pursues a form of political nationalism on the international stage. • This dichotomy between openness and isolationism, cooperation and unilateralism, influences not only domestic policies but also global interactions of BRICS, often creating complex and contradictory scenarios in their international relations.

30. Human Rights and Democracy: • BRICS present a varied picture regarding respect for human rights and democratic principles. While countries like Brazil and South Africa have a history of democratic transition, China and Russia are often criticized for their authoritarian approach. • Differences in political systems and human rights norms often pose obstacles in relations with other countries and affect the ability of BRICS to present a united front on various international issues.

31. Migration and Refugees: • Migration flows and refugee issues are critical themes in the international relations of BRICS. India has faced significant challenges related to refugee crises with neighboring countries, while Brazil has witnessed significant migration flows from Venezuela. • Managing migration, both internal and international, and responding to refugee crises touch on various aspects of BRICS' policies, including development, security, and relations with neighboring countries and the entire international community.

These aspects provide a lens through which to observe the complexity of BRICS' international relations, where national policies, global trends, and regional specificities converge in a complex and often contradictory matrix. Navigating through these diverse, and at times conflicting, themes and dynamics offers a rich and multifaceted landscape that requires further research and detailed analysis to fully understand the role and impact of BRICS in the current global context.

Conclusion on "International Relations and the BRICS": As BRICS continue to emerge as significant powers on the global stage, their interrelationships and relations with other global actors remain a multi-layered set of collaboration, competition, and at times, conflict. Their foreign policy trajectories are heavily influenced by their respective national identities, global aspirations, and the geopolitical and geo-economic dynamics of the contemporary world. In a rapidly evolving world marked by increasing polarization and new global challenges such as climate change, pandemics, and refugee crises, the BRICS coalition embodies a unique reality, rooted in its own contradictions and internal disparities, yet rich in potential in terms of shaping the future of the world order.

• **Role in International Organizations:** • Despite maintaining a critical stance toward the existing international order and its institutions, BRICS are deeply immersed in the dynamics of major global and regional organizations, actively contributing to the creation of global norms and the development of new multilateral platforms and forums. • **Natural Resources and Sustainability:** • Issues related to access to and management of natural resources, as well as challenges related to sustainability and climate change, not only shape the national policies of BRICS but also influence their interaction with the rest of the world, pushing for a dialogue between economic development, energy security, and environmental sustainability.

Global Governance and "Soft Power": • In terms of global governance and the exercise of "soft power," BRICS present themselves as an alternative, proposing models and practices that reflect their specific experiences and visions, thus asserting a plurality of voices and political and economic choices on the world stage.

Technology and Cybersecurity: • The growing relevance of technology-related issues, digitalization, and cybersecurity highlights the strategic importance of innovation and cybersecurity in BRICS' international relations, with implications ranging from economic development to national security and the protection of human rights.

Cooperation vs. Divergence: • While united by a common interest in reimagining the global order, internal divergences on key issues such as democracy, governance, and global strategic alliances represent a critical point that could both weaken the bloc's unity and generate new forms of collaboration and synergy among members.

The landscape of BRICS' international relations thus appears as a complex fabric, where aspirations for global leadership blend with a pragmatic management of emerging challenges and opportunities. The road toward a more equitable and balanced world order, one that takes into account the voices and interests of a broader range of actors, inevitably passes through a deeper and more nuanced understanding of these emerging actors and their impact on global political mechanisms.

In this regard, a more detailed and inclusive analysis of BRICS' international relations requires an approach that goes beyond the simple dynamics of power and considers a plurality of factors and dimensions, including the aspirations of civil society, regional dynamics, and the role of norms and ideas in shaping foreign policies and global interactions.

Understanding their role and impact cannot be divorced from an analysis that takes into account the complexity and multidimensionality of the factors at play, thereby offering a richer and more differentiated framework for the possible future trajectories of BRICS and the international system as a whole.

5. New World Order • Definitions and Key Concepts of the New World Order:

The concept of the "New World Order" is extremely broad and can be analyzed from multiple perspectives. In general terms, it refers to a phase or vision of a renewed international system characterized by different dynamics, rules, and actors compared to traditional ones. Here are some focal points that can provide insights for further exploration and discussion on this topic:

1. **Definitions and Interpretations:**

   - Understand various definitions and interpretations of the "New World Order" from different angles and international theories.

   - Analyze post-Cold War changes, the decline of bipolarity, and the growing multipolarity as a backdrop for the emergence of new actors and dynamics on the international stage.

2. **Global Power Polarity:**

   - Examine the transition from a unipolar/multipolar order to alternative scenarios and what this implies in terms of global power balancing.

   - Explore the role of the United States, China, and other emerging power centers in shaping the new global architecture.

3. **Institutions and Global Governance:**

   - Explore the role of existing institutions (such as the UN, IMF, World Bank) and whether and how they adapt to changing global dynamics.

   - Assess the emergence of new institutions and multilateral platforms, such as BRICS, and their impact on global governance.

4. **Economy and Globalization:**

   - Evaluate how globalization trends and the rise of new economic actors have contributed to reconfiguring the global economy.

- Analyze how the new world order addresses issues such as inequality, resource access, and the management of economic crises.

5. **Security and Conflicts:**

- Examine how security issues are addressed in this new context: non-traditional threats, asymmetric warfare, terrorism, cybersecurity, etc.

- Investigate existing and potential conflicts and tensions among various global and regional powers.

6. **Technology and Information:**

- Analyze the role of new technologies and digital media in shaping politics, economics, and societies on a global level.

- Explore issues of cybersecurity, industrial espionage, and cyber warfare in the new world order.

7. **Human Rights and Democracy:**

- Explore the role of promoting human rights and democracy in the new world order.

- Analyze how different political regimes and ideologies coexist and interact at the international level.

8. **Environment and Sustainability:**

- Examine how environmental challenges, climate change, and sustainability issues are integrated into global policies.

- Analyze how sustainable development strategies intersect with global economic and political dynamics.

These themes represent only some of the crucial aspects to explore the complexity of the concept of the "New World Order." Each point could be further developed, including detailed case studies, comparative analysis, and theoretical insights to provide a comprehensive and multifaceted overview of the subject. Furthermore, the interconnection between these different themes will require an analysis that can grasp the complexity of global interdependencies in this emerging international context.

Socio-Cultural and Ideological Aspects of the New World Order

9. Identity and Nationalism: • Explore the interaction between globalization and national identities, examining how nationalism manifests in the context of the new world order. • Analyze how new global alliances and conflicts influence identity constructions within nations and how this can impact global geopolitics.

10. Social Movements: • Evaluate the role of global social movements, such as those advocating for social, economic, and environmental justice, within the dynamics of the new world order. • Explore how these movements can influence international politics and on which global platforms they operate.

11. Culture and Soft Power: • Delve into the concept of "soft power" and how culture and values are used by states and non-state entities to exert influence on a global scale. • Investigate the implications of cultural diffusion and competition among different "cultures" or "civilizations" within the new global context.

12. Religion and Geopolitics: • Analyze the role of religions and religious identities in shaping international dynamics, including conflicts, alliances, and foreign policies. • Explore the tension between secular and religious principles in global and local governance.

Legal and Normative Aspects

13. International Law: • Evaluate how international law adapts and is implemented within the new world order, considering topics such as sovereignty, humanitarian law, and maritime law. • Examine existing and potential legal mechanisms for conflict resolution and international dispute management.

14. Norms and Standards: • Analyze how global norms and standards (e.g., in human rights, environment, technology, etc.) are established, implemented, and enforced. • Explore how different global visions and values converge in the creation of international norms.

Health and Scientific Aspects

15. Global Health: • Investigate how global health issues, such as pandemics and public health, are managed and how they influence stability and international cooperation. • Analyze the implications of global health crises on international politics, economy, and society.

16. Science and Innovation: • Examine the role of science and technological innovation in shaping the new world order, including ethical, legal, and social issues that arise. • Evaluate how scientific and technological competition and collaboration are integrated into national and international strategies.

Regional and Sub-Regional Dynamics

17. Regional Integration: • Analyze the dynamics and impacts of regional formations and integrations (e.g., EU, ASEAN, MERCOSUR) within the broader global context. • Examine how these regional blocs influence and are influenced by the new world order.

18. Regional Conflict and Cooperation: • Study how regional and sub-regional conflicts and cooperation develop and interact with global dynamics. • Evaluate the dynamics between regional powers and non-state actors (such as terrorist organizations or drug cartels) in shaping local and global order.

Global Interconnections and Resonances

19. Transnationalism: • Explore the role of transnational actors, such as multinational corporations and NGOs, in creating, influencing, and challenging the global order. • Analyze how these entities cooperate and conflict with states and international institutions.

20. Casus Belli and Pacification: • Investigate how the causes of conflicts change, persist, or evolve in the new world order. • Examine mechanisms and tools for post-conflict peacebuilding and stabilization and their applicability in different contexts.

Each of the above-mentioned themes requires in-depth elaboration and critical discussion based on theories, empirical data, concrete examples, and scenario analyses. The potential for elaborating on each of these themes is vast and will require careful research and analysis to provide a clear and multidimensional understanding of the "New World Order."

The concept of the "New World Order" is intricate and multifaceted, nuanced by the different geopolitical and sociocultural perspectives that intersect with it. First and foremost, it is essential to examine the ideological conceptions that delineate the idea of the new world order: understanding how different actors, states, and non-states, perceive it and how they materialize it in their political and strategic agendas.

One of the key aspects worth further exploration concerns the global balance of power. In a context where global balances are shifting, the emergence of BRICS powers (Brazil, Russia, India, China, South Africa) provides an interesting focal point for analyzing how new power dynamics are redefining international relations. The increasing influence of these countries has generated new alliances, not only among themselves but also with other emerging nations, and has stimulated new dynamics within international institutions such as the United Nations, the International Monetary Fund, and the World Bank.

At a broader level, the new world order can be seen through the lens of "the West versus the Rest." The term "the West" here can be understood as a construct that represents not only a geographical location but also a set of values, norms, and political and economic systems, which are often seen in opposition or competition with other "civilizations" or political-economic systems. The growing influence of countries like China, with its model of capitalist authoritarianism, or Russia, with its assertive approach to geopolitics, challenges the previous dominance of Western nations and their liberal ideologies.

Another element worth exploring is the role of emerging technologies and innovation in shaping the new world order. The race for technological leadership in fields such as artificial intelligence, biotechnology, and space technology is crucial for gaining an advantage in terms of soft and hard power on the global stage. BRICS nations, for example, are heavily investing in these areas to secure their place in the future global geopolitical landscape.

On the other hand, environmental and climate issues offer another prism through which to observe transformations in the world order. The increasing urgency of global climate challenges, combined with ambitions for sustainable development, shapes new alliances and generates new conflicts. The management of natural resources, access and control over them, and strategies for mitigating and adapting to climate change all become crucial dimensions through which nations seek to navigate and negotiate their place in the international system.

Furthermore, it is essential to observe how national identities and related identity issues influence the perception and participation in the new world order. Domestic policies, ideological orientations, and the construction of a country's national identity contribute significantly to defining how it positions itself and interacts with other global actors. This, in turn, can be used to examine how BRICS nations are using their growing influence to redefine global power narratives and structures.

The discourse on the new world order and the role of BRICS inevitably leads us to consider the globalized socio-economic context and the global governance system. A critical element in this regard concerns how globalization and its dynamics influence both established and emerging powers. For example, how do BRICS nations navigate the global economic system, which has, in part, been structured and led by established nations and power blocs? And how do their development and industrialization strategies influence the redistribution of wealth and power at the global level?

Additionally, one cannot overlook the role of digitization in the contemporary world order. The digital era has permeated every aspect of society and global governance, influencing both national and international politics, economics, and society. Digitization, through phenomena such as cyberspace and cyber security, has opened new fronts of cooperation and conflict. BRICS nations have shown significant interest in the development of digital technologies, not only as tools for economic progress but also as mechanisms for influencing geopolitics and ensuring national security.

Similarly, the socio-cultural dimension of the new world order is equally pervasive and complex. BRICS nations, with their unique identities and cultures, engage with the international system not only through economic or political lenses but also through the promotion and interaction of their cultures and values. The intersection of geopolitics and culture, often manifested through soft power, is crucial for understanding how national identities are projected and perceived in the international context.

Another significant point of consideration is the issue of security. The concept of security has undergone significant evolution, especially in relation to the challenges posed by the digital environment and new power dynamics. While traditional security challenges, such as territorial conflicts and geopolitical rivalries, remain relevant, new issues such as cyber security, environmental security, and global health security have forcefully entered the international agenda. The recent COVID-19 pandemic, for example, has highlighted the vulnerability of the global system and the importance of building resilience and response capabilities to cross-cutting and interconnected challenges.

It is also essential to explore the theme of the legitimacy and effectiveness of international institutions in the context of the new world order. How do the BRICS perceive and interact with existing international institutions? How do they seek to reform or create new ones to reflect and support their interests and visions? These are key aspects that define their strategy in shaping a world order that is favorable to them.

Finally, but no less important, global inequalities, both among nations and within them, play a fundamental role in determining the dynamics of the new world order. How do the BRICS address issues of inequality and social justice, both nationally and internationally? And how do these dynamics influence their position and strategy in the global context? Their domestic and foreign policies reflect and respond to these critical issues, creating new dynamics and tensions that warrant in-depth analysis in the context of the new world order.

Further deepening the theme of the new world order and the position of BRICS within it, it is crucial to consider climate change and environmental sustainability as decisive drivers of development and international cooperation. How these countries manage their environmental obligations and pursue sustainability goals has profound implications for their interaction with the international community and their global leadership profile.

Climate change, for example, is a field that concerns not only ecological issues but also social, economic, and geopolitical matters. The implications of choices regarding energy policies, biodiversity protection, and natural resource management are essential aspects of the international projection of the BRICS. The energy transition toward cleaner sources, adaptation to climate change, and mitigation of its effects are issues that intersect various sectors, creating new opportunities and challenges for these countries.

Furthermore, the issue of human rights and democratic governance represents another element to examine in the discourse on the BRICS and the new world order. The protection of human rights and the promotion of democracy are central themes in the international debate, and the BRICS, with their diverse realities and approaches regarding civil and political rights, significantly contribute to defining and, in some cases, reshaping global narratives and practices. How they address issues such as freedom of expression, minority rights, and social justice not only affects their international position and reputation but also defines internal and external dynamics and power balances.

It is also relevant to explore how BRICS diplomacy has evolved in the context of South-South dynamics and in relation to development challenges. Cooperation and competition relationships among countries in the Global South present unique dynamics that deserve analysis to understand how the BRICS navigate this context and seek to position themselves as leaders in South-South dynamics. Development assistance, infrastructure investments, technological cooperation, and political solidarity are all aspects that characterize the role of the BRICS in South-South relations.

Additionally, the interaction of the BRICS with other regional and international alliances and blocs is essential to understand how they position themselves in the global landscape. How they engage with organizations such as the United Nations, the International Monetary Fund, the World Bank, and other regional and international blocs and initiatives (such as the European Union, ASEAN, CELAC, etc.) shapes the context in which their strategies and policies take shape and are implemented.

In addition, the role of the BRICS in international crises and in peacekeeping and peacebuilding processes is a significant aspect that greatly impacts their interaction dynamics and global perceptions. How do they position themselves in conflict situations? What is their approach to crisis resolution and peacebuilding? These questions are vital to understanding the nature of their engagement in global governance and to analyzing their influence in the international security and peace architecture.

These aspects, along with those previously discussed, contribute to shaping a complex and multifaceted picture of the role of the BRICS in the new world order. Each explored dimension opens up new possibilities for analysis and understanding of the dynamics characterizing the international system and the strategies of its key actors.

Further exploring the concept of the New World Order (NWO) and the position of the BRICS within this context, there is a need to examine a key element: the geopolitics of emerging technologies and innovation. Technological innovation, especially in areas such as artificial intelligence, biotechnology, renewable energy, and digital technologies, is becoming a crucial battleground for global competition. The BRICS, collectively possessing immense human resources, scientific research capabilities, and market potential, are playing an increasingly prominent role in this context.

The discourse surrounding digitization and technological innovation has profound implications for the global order, suggesting the emergence of a "new technological arms race" in which global and emerging powers compete to establish norms, standards, and governance architectures in cyberspace and emerging technologies. The BRICS represent a heterogeneous bloc in this context, with members like China being global leaders in various technological sectors, while other member countries are navigating and asserting their interests and values in this rapidly evolving environment.

Furthermore, the evolution of the concept of security, which now encompasses not only traditional military threats but also challenges such as pandemics, cyber security, and climate change, demands a reconsideration of strategies and alliances. The BRICS, through mechanisms like the New Development Bank, are seeking to define and implement collaborative and supportive approaches to address these multidimensional threats, reflecting their aspirations for a fairer and more inclusive world order.

Another key aspect is the concept of multilateralism and its evolution in the current context. The BRICS support a multilateralism that better reflects the realities and power balances of the 21st century, one that considers the growing influence of non-Western actors and aspires to a more balanced and representative international system. This implies not only active participation in existing multilateral institutions but also the creation and support of new initiatives and platforms, such as the aforementioned

BRICS New Development Bank and other multilateral and plurilateral initiatives.

Culture and society are equally vital in defining the global positions of the BRICS and their role in the new world order. Social, cultural, and ethnic dynamics within these countries and how they interact with foreign and global policies, as well as interactions between civil society, the private sector, and government, are essential for understanding the motivations, strategies, and impact of the BRICS on the international stage. The BRICS are homes to rich cultural and societal diversities, and their national identities and narratives are intrinsically linked to their external projection and their perception and interaction with the global order.

Finally, the ethics and values that guide the foreign policies of the BRICS and their approach to global governance are critical for deciphering their agenda and trajectory in the new world order. Being a heterogeneous bloc with different political systems, values, and priorities, the BRICS offer fertile ground to explore how different concepts of justice, equity, development, and security translate into concrete policies and cooperation initiatives and how these are negotiated and harmonized within the bloc.

These and many other aspects contribute to creating a complex and nuanced mosaic of the role of the BRICS in the context of the new world order, requiring a thorough and multi-dimensional assessment that takes into account the numerous intersections and implications of the various dynamics at play.

The concept of the New World Order (NWO) is closely intertwined with the global geopolitical and socio-economic context. Examining the role of the BRICS in this landscape, it is essential to consider how these countries interpret and influence the ongoing changes and, more broadly, the restructuring of the international scene.

In this context, the importance of soft power strategies and cultural influence cannot be underestimated. The BRICS, each with a distinct and significant cultural heritage, are increasingly using their cultural resources as tools to project power and influence globally. Cinema, art, music, and other forms of cultural expression become vehicles through which these countries communicate their values, histories, and worldviews, thus seeking to shape global narratives and perceptions.

Each member of the BRICS has developed, to varying degrees, soft power strategies to elevate its status and strengthen its international agendas. For example, China has expanded its network of global cultural and educational institutions, such as Confucius Institutes, promoting Chinese language and culture worldwide. Similarly, Brazil has used its cultural and sporting charisma (think of football and Carnival) to enhance its international brand.

When discussing the NWO, it is also crucial to consider the concept of "global justice" and how the BRICS view and navigate this concept in relation to their national interests and objectives. BRICS countries have often emphasized the need for a fairer and more just world order that addresses structural inequalities and provides opportunities and a voice to developing countries.

The issue of sustainable development is another key element in the analysis of BRICS-NWO dynamics. The BRICS are central to debates on sustainable development due to their significant environmental impact and the challenges they face in terms of development and growth. Natural resource management, energy transition, and environmental policies are critical issues that these emerging economies must address, both nationally and as part of their international agenda and responsibilities.

Vaccine diplomacy in the context of the COVID-19 pandemic is another relevant example of the position of the BRICS in the new world order. The pandemic has highlighted both divisions and opportunities for international cooperation. Countries like China and Russia have used vaccine supply as a diplomatic tool, seeking to increase their influence and partnerships through vaccine distribution in various regions of the world.

It is also essential to explore the dimensions of security and defense in the BRICS-NWO context. How BRICS countries perceive and address security threats, both regionally and globally, and how they coordinate and cooperate on these issues are vital to understanding their roles and influences in the global landscape.

Furthermore, the nature and dynamics of international coalitions and alliances are central to shaping the future prospects of the NWO and the position of the BRICS within it. In a world where tensions among major global powers are increasing, alliances and partnerships are being redefined and evolving.

Continuing to explore and probe these and other themes will provide a deep and nuanced understanding of how the BRICS navigate, shape, and are shaped by the emerging global power geometry.

The analysis of the BRICS and the New World Order (NWO) leads us to probe further facets of the presence and influence of these countries on the international stage. Technology, cybersecurity, and digitization are crucial aspects to explore when discussing the posture of these nations within the global power geometry.

The role of the BRICS in the digital age is particularly significant in an increasingly interconnected world. China, for example, has positioned itself as a digital superpower, investing heavily in technologies such as artificial intelligence, 5G, and blockchain. Its Digital Silk Road Initiative aims to extend its digital influence globally by connecting telecommunications infrastructure, developing e-commerce and digital finance projects, and promoting its vision of cyberspace on the international stage.

India, with its highly connected population and rapidly growing IT sector, is also a significant player in the digital domain. The country faces challenges and opportunities arising from being one of the largest digital democracies, including data privacy issues, internet governance, and digitalization of the economy.

Russia, with its expertise in cybersecurity and active presence in cyberspace, plays an influential role in the global cybersecurity landscape. Its capabilities in cyber intelligence and cyber defense are relevant when discussing the dynamics of the NWO and global cyber-political tensions.

Cryptocurrencies and digital finance are another important theme that intersects the BRICS and the NWO. China has launched its own digital currency, while other BRICS countries are actively exploring the opportunities and challenges of digital financial technologies and cryptocurrencies. The digitization of finance has the potential to reshape the global economy, offering new mechanisms for trade, investment, and economic governance.

Issues related to social justice and inequality are also crucial when discussing the BRICS and the NWO. Each BRICS member faces significant challenges related to inequality, both domestically and internationally. The fight against poverty, the promotion of gender equality, and access to education and healthcare are issues that reflect national agendas and influence the international postures of BRICS countries.

The issue of climate change is fundamental. The BRICS, with India, China, and Brazil among the world's largest polluters, have a significant role to play in the global fight against climate change. Their energy policies, international commitments, and sustainable development strategies are vital components of their international presence and the dynamics of the NWO.

Demographic dynamics and the governance of migration flows are other aspects that intertwine the BRICS and the NWO. The management of both internal and international migrations and the demographic policies of BRICS countries have implications for labor, development, and security at both national and global levels.

Diplomatic strategies and the use of public and cultural diplomacy by the BRICS, their national narratives, and the image they project internationally are vital for understanding how these nations influence and are influenced by the emerging new world order.

In this complex and multi-faceted scenario, the BRICS continue to navigate, actively contributing to shaping and being shaped by the dynamics and transformations of the new world order. Continuing to explore these and other interconnected themes reveals a complex and multifaceted picture of the presence of the BRICS in the current and future international context.

Continuing the analysis of the New World Order (NWO) and the BRICS, the focus now turns specifically to the realm of international security and geopolitics. Given their growing economic and political influence, the BRICS are increasingly key actors in global power dynamics, and their influence extends to issues ranging from security to defense, human rights to climate change.

The challenge to global governance posed by the BRICS is highlighted by their attempts to balance the promotion of existing norms and institutions with the introduction of new ideas and platforms. For example, the BRICS Development Bank represents an attempt by these nations to create an alternative to existing international financial institutions such as the International Monetary Fund and the World Bank.

The concept of sovereignty, especially in the context of cyberspace and information technology, is crucial when discussing the BRICS and the NWO. The growing digitization and transition to a global knowledge-based economy entail the reformulation of international norms, policies, and laws. The BRICS, with their various capabilities and approaches to digital technology and cybersecurity, significantly influence the structure of the global cyberspace, with China and Russia, for example, promoting a concept of "digital sovereignty."

The concepts of peace and security are equally essential in exploring the position of the BRICS in the NWO. The perception and projection of military power, as well as the approach to conflict resolution and mediation, underline the fundamental philosophies of these states regarding international security. Cooperation and competition in contexts such as the Indian Ocean and the Pacific, as well as aspects of energy security, represent areas where the policies and strategies of the BRICS profoundly influence geopolitics and global power dynamics.

The issue of global inequalities, both among BRICS countries themselves and between the BRICS and other nations, is another crucial aspect. Balancing economic growth and sustainability, the fight against poverty, and social inclusion represent a fundamental dimension of the global presence of the BRICS. Each member country faces specific and diverse challenges, but the tension between prosperity and equality is a common theme that runs through their national and international agendas.

Themes of innovation and technological development are critical to understanding how the BRICS are positioning themselves on the global stage. Competition, but also collaboration in the field of research and development, artificial intelligence, biotechnology, and other areas of technological innovation, will be decisive in determining the future influence of these countries on the NWO.

The cultural and social dimension is another key element when examining the role of the BRICS in the global context. The promotion of culture, values, and social norms through means such as cultural diplomacy and media platforms is an essential component of international influence.

In every context, BRICS nations find themselves navigating a complex mosaic of challenges and opportunities, seeking dynamic balances between their national agendas and international commitments and pressures. Their trajectories, influenced by both internal and external factors, will not only shape the future development paths of these nations but also the form and substance of the emerging new world order (NWO) in the near future.

Exploring the New World Order (NWO) and the role of BRICS within it inevitably raises questions about how these five nations (Brazil, Russia, India, China, and South Africa) can cooperate and compete with existing institutions and how their actions can redefine the global architecture of governance.

Examining the phenomenon of the NWO requires a careful evaluation of its structure, which is driven not only by politics but also by economic, social, technological, and cultural factors. The NWO is often perceived as a system in which global power and influence are distributed in a more heterogeneous and multipolar manner, involving non-state actors such as international organizations, multinational corporations, and civil society groups, which play an increasingly significant role.

The BRICS, with their rapidly growing economies and large populations, represent a significant force within this new paradigm. However, each country has a unique approach to the NWO based on its own needs, goals, and national challenges.

For example, China is often seen as a key player in shaping a new NWO paradigm. Through initiatives like the Belt and Road Initiative (BRI), Beijing has sought to redefine its position in global geopolitics, emphasizing cooperation and connectivity over dominance. China is also striving to establish itself as a leader in global dialogues on issues such as climate change and sustainability.

India, with its pluralistic democracy and rapidly growing economy, represents another vital pole within the BRICS. The country has actively pursued a multilateral agenda, actively participating in international forums and initiatives, and strives to balance relations with key actors like the United States and China. India's challenge is to skillfully navigate between economic cooperation and geopolitical tensions, particularly in relation to borders and regional security.

Russia, with its projection of military power and energy resources, plays a crucial role in determining the power dynamics of the NWO. Its actions in Ukraine and Syria, as well as its relations with Europe and the United States, continue to shape the security and stability of international politics. Russia is also an active player in the Arctic, a region that is becoming increasingly strategic due to climate change and untapped natural resources.

Brazil, with its rich natural resources and diversified economy, seeks to balance its development needs with environmental responsibility. Deforestation in the

Amazon and the balance between agriculture, industry, and sustainability remain crucial issues for Brazil's position in the NWO, as do its social policies and the management of diversity and inequalities within the country.

South Africa, representing a reference point for the African continent within the BRICS, faces challenges such as inequality, poverty, and the need for structural reforms. The country plays a key role in promoting stability and development in Africa and seeks to balance this with its position and commitments in the broader global context.

All these aspects – from domestic challenges to participation in international forums and bodies, from bilateral relations to multilateral commitments, and from economic governance to the promotion of human rights and sustainable development – represent the building blocks with which the BRICS construct their role in the NWO, continuously seeking to reshape and renegotiate their place within global power and cooperation dynamics.

Continuing to delve into the concept of the New World Order (NWO) and the role of the BRICS, it becomes evident that understanding the strategies, objectives, and methodologies used by these countries to navigate the complex web of international relations and the challenges posed by global geopolitics is crucial. The

BRICS are not just an economic aggregate; they represent a coalition where each member brings its own resources, challenges, and aspirations.

The NWO is not a static and monolithic concept. It is shaped and continually redefined by the changing nature of power balances, ideologies, policies, and economies of the leading nations. The BRICS, each with its own agenda and worldview, seek to influence the NWO in unique and diversified ways.

China, for instance, has implemented a strategy of "debt-trap diplomacy," financing massive infrastructure projects in developing countries while simultaneously creating financial dependence and increasing its geopolitical influence. Its "One Belt, One Road" initiative aims to strengthen and diversify trade routes, reducing dependence on those controlled by Western powers.

India, on the other hand, is striving to enhance its power and influence both in the South Asian region and on the global stage. The country has undertaken initiatives to bolster its maritime presence, improve relations with South Asian neighbors, and build partnerships with other global powers. India's diplomacy operates on a complex terrain where it must balance competition with China and Pakistan while establishing strong relationships with the USA, Russia, and the European Union.

Russia has pursued a foreign policy that often contradicts that of the West. The annexation of Crimea in 2014 and support for regimes like the Syrian one demonstrate a clear divergence from Western policies. Russia uses its energy resources as a tool of political influence while simultaneously seeking to diversify its alliances and trading partners, including both external actors like China and other BRICS members.

Brazil has oscillated between a foreign policy oriented toward multilateralism and periods of focus on national interests. Protecting its vast natural resources, along with economic and social development, is an ongoing challenge. Brazil often seeks to balance its economic growth with the need to protect and preserve the Amazon, a topic that has caused tensions both domestically and internationally.

South Africa has taken a leadership role in the development and integration of Africa. Through the African Union and other regional forums, South Africa aims to address issues like security, sustainable development, and economic cooperation while facing internal challenges such as economic inequalities, social issues, and the need for stable and inclusive growth.

Exploring these aspects, it becomes clear that the BRICS are both collaborators and rivals, both on a bilateral level and within the multilateral context of the

NWO. The challenge in the future will be to navigate through these dynamics, manage tensions, and build a dialogue that promotes not only national interests but also sustainable global cooperation and development. In this framework, the concept of the NWO continues to evolve, influenced by the trajectories and interactions of these significant actors on the world stage.

The concept of the New World Order, being as elastic as it is complex, transcends mere geopolitical or economic constructs, delving into the realms of ideology, culture, and international norms. Its realization, or even its configuration, varies significantly depending on the lenses through which it is observed: the Western capitalist, the socialist, the authoritarian, or the global South development theorist, each will have a different view of what the NWO represents or should represent.

Contrary to a monolithic Western entity, the BRICS offer a palette of approaches to globalization, sovereignty, democracy, development, and international security. This diversity, both in terms of internal challenges and external objectives, represents both an opportunity and a challenge for shaping an emerging world order.

The dynamics of the New World Order will largely be defined by how the BRICS powers negotiate their bilateral and multilateral relationships with the West, as well as with each other. The articulation of their domestic agendas with international expectations and pressures will play a key role in this context.

China, with its massive economic weight and growing military presence, will continue to be a key agent of change in the NWO, seeking to reshape global norms and institutions in favor of a system that better reflects its national interests and values. Its relationship with India, in particular, will be crucial, as both nations aspire to greater global influence but are also entangled in regional issues and unresolved bilateral security concerns.

India, on the other hand, will maneuver in a position of power balance between adherence to a rules-based liberal order and the need to manage a complex and sometimes conflictual relationship with China. Its adherence to democratic principles places it in a unique context among the BRICS, which often lean towards state authoritarianism or illiberal democracy.

Russia, isolated by Western sanctions and driven towards greater internal authoritarianism and foreign activism, navigates between the need to cooperate with China and India and protect its interests in the former Soviet republics, an area it considers of vital national interest.

Brazil and South Africa, both regional powers with significant internal challenges, will be key actors in defining how the Global South, particularly Africa and Latin America, positions itself in the context of the NWO. Their ability to balance domestic economic development, environmental sustainability, and international community expectations will define their influence and leadership not only in their respective regions but also in the broader context of the NWO.

In conclusion, the NWO and the role of the BRICS within it will be heavily influenced by the internal and external dynamics of these countries, their interactions with each other, and their relationships with other global and regional powers. A complex interplay of cooperation and conflict, convergence and divergence of interests and values, will shape the global stage in the coming years and decades. The depth and substance of discourse and analysis on these issues will therefore be essential for understanding and navigating the complex and evolving landscape of the future world order.

6. Impact of BRICS on the New World Order

The BRICS, both collectively and as individual actors, play a crucial role in shaping the New World Order (NWO), not only due to their economic strength but also through their geopolitical weight and foreign policies.

A. Global Economic Significance

1. **Economic Influence:** The combined economies of BRICS hold significant global sway, and economic decisions made by these countries often have repercussions far beyond their borders.

2. **Direct Investments:** BRICS serve as sources and destinations for substantial foreign direct investments, contributing to establishing economic ties with various regions of the world.

3. **Trade:** The increase in intra-BRICS trade and trade with other nations influences global trade dynamics, creating new routes and altering existing balances.

B. Contribution to Global Governance

1. **Multilateral Institutions:** BRICS' participation in and sometimes contestation of existing multilateral institutions highlight their desire to reform global governance.

2. **Creation of New Platforms:** The establishment of new platforms and institutions, such as the BRICS Development Bank, indicates an interest in creating alternatives to traditional Western mechanisms.

C. Approach to Sovereignty and Interventionism

1. **Principle of Non-Interference:** Their common commitment to the principle of non-interference in internal affairs informs their approach to international issues.

2. **Response to Conflicts:** BRICS' stance on conflicts and international crises often opposes that of Western powers, offering alternatives or contrasting proposed solutions.

D. Regional and Bilateral Dynamics

1. **Bilateral Relations:** Bilateral relations among BRICS members and other nations influence global alliances and conflicts.

2. **Regional Leadership:** How BRICS influence and manage their respective regions also determines the evolution of global power.

E. Global Security Issues

1. **Security Policy:** BRICS are vital in addressing security issues such as nuclear proliferation, cyber-security, and terrorism.

2. **Military Cooperation:** Intra-BRICS military cooperation and cooperation with other nations can influence power balances and establish new security coalitions.

F. Environmental and Climate Challenges

1. **Climate Change:** Given their scale, BRICS' environmental policies are crucial in shaping global efforts against climate change.

2. **Sustainability:** The economic growth of BRICS raises questions about sustainability and the balance between development and conservation.

G. Disparities and Socio-Economic Development • Growth and Inequality:

The economic growth of BRICS has brought significant benefits but has also led to inequalities within and among countries, raising issues of balancing economic expansion with social justice and poverty reduction. • **Migrations:** Economic attractiveness and opportunities in BRICS drive both internal and international migration, influencing demographic and social dynamics that, in turn, impact policies and international relations.

**H. Innovation and Global Competitiveness •
Technology and Digitalization:** The digital
revolution and technological innovation in BRICS not
only bolster their economies but also create new
challenges in terms of regulations, security, and global
competitiveness.

• Education and Research: Investments in
education and research are crucial to maintaining and
enhancing BRICS' global competitiveness, requiring in-
depth analysis of how these areas influence and are
influenced by international dynamics.

I. Demographic and Societal Issues

• Aging and Youth: Various demographic nuances
within BRICS, such as aging societies and youthful
populations, create a matrix of challenges and
opportunities that influence domestic policies and
international relations.

• Culture and Identity: Cultural diversity and
identity issues within BRICS are relevant for
understanding domestic political trajectories and how
they intersect with foreign policy and international
relations.

J. Health Policies and Pandemics

• Global Health: BRICS play a pivotal role in global
health policies, and the management of health crises

like the COVID-19 pandemic underscores the importance of international cooperation and health governance.

• **Healthcare Access and Innovation:** Access to healthcare services and medical innovations influence and are influenced by global economic and political dynamics in which BRICS are deeply intertwined.

K. Power Dynamics and Leadership

• **Soft Power:** The exercise of soft power through culture, media, and international relations by BRICS is a field deserving of thorough analysis to understand its implications for global power dynamics.

• **International Leadership:** How BRICS exert leadership and influence international norms in various fields, from environment to human rights, is crucial for grasping future trajectories of the NWO.

L. Resources and Environment

• **Resource Management:** Policies and practices related to the management of natural resources in BRICS not only affect their economies but also global ones, with implications for security, cooperation, and conflict.

• **Environmental Policies:** BRICS play a central role in global environmental dynamics, and their approach to climate and environmental policies will be crucial in addressing ecological challenges in the future.

Le BRICS, attraverso tutte queste dimensioni, sono attori fondamentali nel modellare le dinamiche globali, sia in termini di economia che di geopolitica. La loro crescita, le sfide interne, e il modo in cui gestiscono le loro politiche esterne, diventano, quindi, di vitale importanza per comprendere e analizzare l'evoluzione del nuovo ordine mondiale. Esaminare ciascuna di queste aree con uno sguardo critico e analitico consentirà di comprendere meglio il ruolo e l'impatto delle BRICS nel contesto globale più ampio, gettando luce su potenziali scenari futuri e sulle sfide che il mondo affronterà nei prossimi anni e decenni.

6. Impact of BRICS on the New World Order

A. Multilateralism and International Institutions • Institutional Interactions: BRICS, with their collective influence, interact with, challenge, and sometimes seek to reform existing international institutions like the UN, IMF, and World Bank to better reflect and accommodate their interests and priorities.

• Multilateral Cooperation: They often aim to balance the unilateralism of some powers with enhanced multilateral cooperation, striving for greater equity and representation in the international system.

B. South-South Cooperation

• **Economic and Political Ties:** BRICS actively work to develop and strengthen economic and political ties among countries in the Global South, providing an alternative to the traditional dominance of Western powers.

• **Dialogue Platforms:** They create and utilize dialogue and cooperation platforms, such as the BRICS Summit, to promote South-South collaboration and advance shared agendas on global issues.

C. Building New Structures

• **Economic Initiatives:** BRICS are actively involved in constructing new structures and economic initiatives, such as the New Development Bank, which aims to offer financing alternatives for development projects in the developing world.

• **Networks of Trade:** They seek to establish networks of trade and investments that can diversify their economies, reduce dependence on Western powers, and enhance mutual economic resilience.

D. Security and Defense Policy

• **Regional Stability:** BRICS are actively engaged in seeking to maintain and, in some cases, stabilize the regions in which they are situated, addressing challenges like terrorism, piracy, and regional conflicts.
• **Security Cooperation:** They also explore areas of security and defense cooperation, balancing their national security policies with the need to address collective and transnational challenges.

E. Investment and Development Strategies

• **Direct Investments:** BRICS have become significant sources of foreign direct investments, influencing economic development in many regions through infrastructure financing, job creation, and increased trade.

• **Economic Influence:** By investing in developing countries, they also increase their economic and political influence, shaping global and regional power dynamics.

F. Promotion of Values and Norms •
Development Models: BRICS offer alternative models of development and governance that often contrast with those proposed by Western liberal democracies, challenging existing paradigms on issues

like global governance and sustainable development. • **Values and Principles:** While promoting non-interference and sovereignty respect, BRICS' actions also reflect and shape emerging global norms, influencing international rules and practices.

G. Changes in Global Trade • Supply Chains: BRICS significantly influence global supply chains, not only as major producers and exporters but also through the creation and development of new markets and trade partnerships. • **New Trade Routes:** By investing in global infrastructure, such as China's Belt and Road Initiative, they are also reshaping trade routes and transportation networks, affecting the global economy and power dynamics.

H. Global Challenges and Solutions • Climate Change: As some of the largest polluters and resource consumers, BRICS are central to discussions and actions related to climate change, and their energy and environmental policies will have a significant impact on the world's ability to address future ecological crises. • **Global Health:** After the COVID-19 pandemic, managing global health crises and access to global public goods like vaccines have become central, and BRICS' policies and actions in these areas will be crucial in shaping future global health systems.

Through these themes, the impact of BRICS on the New World Order can be examined and understood in multiple dimensions. With their growing influence and complex internal and external dynamics, BRICS continue to play a key role in reshaping global structures and processes, offering new pathways and perspectives, but also presenting new challenges and tensions that require careful analysis and understanding. Their ability to navigate these dynamics, build internal cohesion, and manage effective external relations will be critical to their future impact and role in the international system.

The impact of BRICS in the context of the New World Order remains deeply interconnected with various aspects, including technology policies, cultural diplomacy, and influence in international forums.

Technology and Innovation • Research and Development: The collective BRICS places a strong emphasis on research and development, investing in fields such as artificial intelligence, biotechnology, and renewable energy. Innovations from these countries, such as advancements in vaccine production and the development of green technologies, have a direct impact on the global community. • **Cyber Norms:** In today's digitized world, internet governance and cyber norms are becoming increasingly crucial. As significant markets for digital consumers and influential actors in defining cyber-space norms, BRICS wield considerable influence in global discussions related to cybersecurity and data protection.

Cultural Diplomacy • Soft Power: Cultural diplomacy through soft power represents another vehicle through which BRICS seek to shape the New World Order. Whether it's Bollywood cinema, Brazilian art, or the promotion of the Russian language, efforts to project soft power not only increase their cultural influence but also build bridges and create perceptions across borders. • **Education:** Additionally, education and academic exchanges provide another means through which BRICS build connections and influence global discourse. Universities like Tsinghua in China or IIT in India are becoming increasingly influential in educating the next generation of global leaders.

Global Forums and Platforms • Global Leadership: The presence of BRICS in global forums such as the G20, WTO, and other multilateral spaces is becoming more prominent. Using these platforms, they can influence global economic decisions and shape the agenda on issues like international trade, digital taxation, and sovereign debt. • **Collaboration and Competition:** While BRICS collaborate in some forums and contexts, they also find themselves in situations of competition and rivalry, both among themselves and with other global powers. This dualistic dynamic of collaboration and competition often reflects how BRICS seek to shape and respond to emerging global structures and challenges.

Demographic and Social Changes • Population Dynamics: Demographic dynamics within BRICS, including the challenges of an aging population in countries like China and Russia, contrasted with demographic booms in countries like India, create both opportunities and challenges. The influence of BRICS and their ability to shape the world order are closely interconnected with the management of their internal demographic and social dynamics. • **Social Issues:** Attention to social justice, equality, and inclusive development within BRICS also translates into a range of policies and approaches that can influence global norms and values, as well as their acceptance and implementation of international agreements and development goals.

Natural Resources and Environment • Resource Security: BRICS, rich in resources, play a key role in the management and sustainable use of natural resources, influencing global dynamics related to resource security, environmental management, and climate change. • **Environmental Strategies:** The adoption of green technologies and strategies for mitigating climate change, as well as their commitment to UN Sustainable Development Goals and the goals of the Paris Agreement, will significantly impact global environmental policies and sustainable development dynamics.

This overview, though not exhaustive, shows how BRICS influence and are influenced by the broader context of global dynamics, impacting the shaping of the new world order through various channels and mechanisms. Their trajectory and future decisions will continue to be a crucial factor in defining global trends in the coming decades.

Sustainable Development and Environmental Challenges BRICS, with their rapid and ongoing economic growth, must address various challenges related to environmental sustainability. How these nations confront environmental and sustainable development challenges will have a significant impact on the global environment, given their extensive ecological footprint. • **Environmental Commitment:** BRICS are gradually emerging as key players in international discussions on climate change and biodiversity. Their approaches and commitments to achieving UN Sustainable Development Goals and the goals of the Paris Agreement will greatly influence the future of the planet.

Security and Regional Stability BRICS' security and defense policies, and how they manage regional conflicts and tensions, influence global stability. • **Regional Tensions:** In Asia, for example, power balances and tensions between India and China can shape regional and global geopolitics. Similarly, Russia's relations with its European neighbors and the postures of Brazil and South Africa in their regional contexts are vital dynamics.

Health Cooperation Health cooperation among BRICS has grown, especially in light of the COVID-19 pandemic. • **Pandemic Management:** BRICS' collective approach to managing health crises, vaccine production and distribution, and collaboration in scientific research influence global health and the response to pandemics.

Economic and Trade Integration Economic and trade integration among BRICS is another fundamental aspect. • **Trade Agreements:** The development of bilateral and multilateral trade agreements, and how BRICS engage with other emerging and developed economies, will help define the future of the global economic order.

Anti-Corruption Efforts BRICS have also collectively and individually committed to combating corruption. • **Anti-Corruption Norms:** The adoption and implementation of anti-corruption regulations and laws have an impact not only at the national level but also internationally, influencing global governance and standards in financial and corporate sectors.

Infrastructure Development BRICS are heavily investing in infrastructure development, a vital element for economic growth. • **Infrastructure Initiatives:** China's Belt and Road Initiative, infrastructure projects in India, and similar efforts in Brazil, Russia, and South Africa are not only changing the physical landscape of these nations but also regional economic and geopolitical dynamics.

Innovation in the Financial Sector • BRICS Financial Institutions: The creation of financial institutions like the New Development Bank (NDB) of BRICS is a clear example of the group's desire to shape the global financial architecture and provide alternatives to Western-led institutions.

These dynamics reflect the interconnectedness and mutual influence of BRICS in the global context, showing how their internal and external policies intersect with the challenges and opportunities of the New World Order. BRICS' ability to collaborate, coordinate policies, and build shared solutions to global challenges will be crucial for their future influence on the global stage.

Social Policies and Inequalities • Social Inequity: Within BRICS, income disparity, social inequalities, and challenges related to gender and ethnicity are significant issues that impact their domestic social and economic policies and their approach to international cooperation and development.

Demographic Change BRICS are characterized by diverse demographic trends that, in turn, influence their policies and global perspectives. • **Demographic Dynamics:** India, for example, stands out for its relatively young population and rapid urbanization, while China is dealing with an aging population due in part to its previous one-child policy. These diverse demographic dynamics affect domestic policies and long-term development prospects.

Energy Security • Energy Dependence: Energy security and dependence on fossil fuels, especially in the context of climate change and the evolution of renewable energy, are central issues. Russia is a net energy exporter, while India is one of the world's largest oil importers. These dynamics deeply impact their energy policies and commitment to energy transition.

Culture and Soft Power • Cultural Influence: BRICS are also seeking to expand their cultural influence and global soft power through various means, including media, culture, education, and public diplomacy, in order to increase their impact and attractiveness on the world stage.

Vaccine Diplomacy • Vaccination: The distribution of vaccines, particularly evident during the COVID-19 pandemic, has become a diplomatic tool. China and Russia, for example, have used vaccine supply as a tool of global diplomacy, seeking to increase their influence in strategic regions.

Technology and Cybersecurity • Cyber Warfare: In an era dominated by technology and information, BRICS are also exploring the cyber domain. Cybersecurity and cyber warfare have become crucial issues not only for national security but also for economic stability and daily operations.

Tourism and Cultural Exchanges • Intercultural Exchanges: Tourism and cultural exchanges among BRICS and with other nations represent another mechanism through which these nations seek to enhance mutual understanding and strengthen ties at various levels.

Space Sector Cooperation • Space Exploration: BRICS are also collaborating in the space sector. For example, China and Russia have announced joint plans to build a lunar space station.

With their diverse and complex challenges and opportunities, BRICS will continue to play a fundamental role in shaping the future trajectories of the new world order. How they manage their internal challenges and navigate international dynamics will determine not only their destiny but also have a significant impact on global geopolitics and the global economy in the near future.

Impact of BRICS on the New World Order

BRICS, with their growing economic, political, and military importance, are assuming an increasingly dominant role in the world order. This point can be further developed with particular attention to the following subtopics:

Economic Impact: BRICS are a significant driving force in the global economy, with substantial contributions to global GDP and international trade. The expansion of their economies has influenced international trade and financial dynamics, gradually shifting the global economic center of gravity. For example, China has become the world's second-largest economy and a fundamental pillar of global growth.

Political Leadership: BRICS have become more assertive in exerting their political influence and shaping global governance. Their cooperation in multilateral forums and the formation of alliances (such as the BRICS organization itself) have created new platforms and vehicles for global political action and influence.

Security and Defense: In the military and security domains, BRICS are enhancing their defensive and security capabilities. Their participation and commitment to regional conflicts and global security issues, such as UN peacekeeping missions, are shaping new power balances.

Environment and Sustainability: BRICS, being among the largest greenhouse gas emitters and having a significant ecological footprint, play a crucial role in global environmental dynamics. Their policies and commitments regarding climate change and sustainability are pivotal for the planet's future.

Technology and Innovation: In terms of technology and innovation, BRICS are at the forefront of developing and implementing emerging technologies such as artificial intelligence and biotechnology, influencing global regulations, ethics, and competitive dynamics.

International Relations: BRICS' relations with each other and with other global powers are another crucial aspect. How BRICS interact with nations like the United States, the European Union, and other emerging powers establishes new dynamics and polarizations in the international landscape.

Challenges and Opportunities: Challenges such as internal inequalities, social issues, and political tensions, along with opportunities such as economic growth potential and technological development, define the future paths of BRICS and their impact on the world order.

In conclusion, through their policies, strategies, and global interactions, BRICS are shaping the new world order, influencing global economic, political, and social dynamics. Their collaboration, internal tensions, and external relations create an intricate web of cooperation and competition that will be decisive for the future shape of international politics, economics, and society. Analyzing and understanding the trajectories, strategies, and dynamics of BRICS are essential for deciphering and predicting the evolution of the global landscape in the 21st century.

7. Technology and Innovation • Role of BRICS in technological development and innovation.

Technology and Innovation in BRICS The role of BRICS (Brazil, Russia, India, China, and South Africa) in technological development and innovation is particularly influential and offers a vast and complex landscape to explore, given the diversity and specificities of each member nation. Below are various aspects related to the role of BRICS in the global technological and innovative landscape.

A. Dynamics of Innovation and Technological Development BRICS are significant players in the realm of technological innovation, with a growing global impact.

1. **China:** With its massive industrialization and "Made in China 2025" strategy, the nation aims to become a leader in various high-tech sectors, including artificial intelligence, robotics, information technology, renewable energy, and electric vehicles.

2. **India:** Known for its robust IT sector and innovation in technology services, India has a rapidly growing startup ecosystem and is making strides in biotechnology, space technology, and renewable energy.

3. **Brazil:** Stands out for its research in renewable energy, particularly in bioethanol production and advanced agricultural research, despite challenges in allocating resources to R&D.

4. **Russia:** Has strengths in the aerospace and nuclear sectors and is seeking to diversify its economy by increasing investments in innovation and technology.

5. **South Africa:** Despite facing various challenges, the country plays a significant role in technological development in the African continent, with a focus on information technology, renewable energy, and astronomy.

B. Collaboration and Technological Competition BRICS engage in both cooperation and competition in the fields of innovation and technology, creating a complex network of partnerships and rivalries. • **Cooperation:** There are numerous examples of collaboration among BRICS, such as joint research and development initiatives, scientific conferences, and partnerships in the space sector. • **Competition:** Competition for dominance in key sectors, such as artificial intelligence and telecommunications (e.g., 5G networks), is palpable among BRICS members, particularly between China and India.

C. Global Implications of BRICS Technology and Innovation

The growing influence of BRICS in technology and innovation has several global implications:

- **Global Economy:** Technological innovation in BRICS influences global economic dynamics, offering new market opportunities and creating new centers for production and technological development.

- **Cybersecurity:** Advanced technological capabilities also imply an increasing capacity to influence cyberspace, with BRICS becoming relevant actors in cybersecurity and cyber warfare.

- **Environment:** The development of green technologies and innovative solutions for climate change by BRICS can have a significant impact on global environmental dynamics.

D. Challenges and Opportunities

BRICS face a series of challenges related to innovation, including intellectual property protection, promoting research and development, and nurturing scientific and technological talent.

- **Opportunities:** BRICS can leverage their expertise and resources to catalyze innovation, such as by promoting startups and attracting foreign investments.

- **Challenges:** Issues like equitable technology access, patentability, and ethical considerations in innovation are crucial and represent significant challenges.

In conclusion, BRICS, with their distinctive dynamics of technological development and innovation, shape not only their growth trajectories but also influence the global technological and innovative architecture. The balance between collaboration and competition, internal challenges, and the global implications of their technological ascent form a rich and multifaceted context that deserves in-depth and multifaceted analysis to thoroughly understand the future dynamics of global innovation and technology.

Expanding the Discussion on Technology and Innovation in BRICS

E. Digitalization and the Technology Sector

Digitalization has assumed a prominent role in the economies of BRICS, leading to digital transformation across various sectors. For example, the launch and adoption of digital technologies in BRICS have significantly influenced existing infrastructure and the socio-economic landscape of member countries.

- **Fintech:** The financial technology (Fintech) sector has seen significant development in BRICS countries, especially in China and India, where the advent of digital payment platforms like Alipay and Paytm has revolutionized financial transactions and credit culture.

- **E-commerce:** The e-commerce sector is expanding, with giants like Alibaba and Flipkart dominating local markets and beginning to make international forays.

F. Technological Sustainability

Technological innovation in BRICS countries encompasses not only technological advancement but also its sustainability.

- **Energy:** Sustainable technologies, especially those related to renewable energies, are at the forefront of research and development. China, for instance, is one of the world's leading producers of solar panels.

- **Electric Vehicles:** The adoption and production of electric vehicles are another area where BRICS countries are significantly investing, with the aim of reducing dependence on fossil fuels and limiting CO_2 emissions.

G. Start-up Ecosystem

The start-up landscape in BRICS countries presents a diverse panorama rich in opportunities but also challenges.

- **Innovation in Entrepreneurship:** While centers like Bangalore and Shenzhen are recognized as innovation hubs, obstacles like bureaucracy and access to funding remain challenges that startups must face in these countries.

- **Investments:** The availability of venture capital, angel investors, and incubators has played a crucial role in nurturing the startup ecosystem, although investment dynamics vary considerably among BRICS countries.

H. Digital Inclusion and Disparities

Despite rapid digitalization, a significant portion of the population in BRICS countries remains excluded from the benefits of the digital revolution.

- **Technology Access:** Disparities in access to the internet and digital technologies between urban and rural areas persist, affecting the equity of technological innovation.

- **Digital Literacy:** Digital literacy is another challenge, with a significant portion of the population lacking the necessary skills to navigate the digital world.

I. Research and Development (R&D)

Research and development (R&D) are fundamental components of innovation, and BRICS countries are seeking to increase their investments in this area.

- **International Collaboration:** There are numerous examples of collaboration in R&D both within the BRICS bloc and with other countries and international organizations.

- **Brexit and Innovation:** Countries like India and China have explored new opportunities for R&D collaboration with the United Kingdom post-Brexit, creating new channels for scientific and technological exchange.

J. Biotechnology and Health

BRICS countries are also exploring the field of biotechnology, with a particular focus on healthcare.

- **Vaccines:** The COVID-19 pandemic has highlighted the importance of biotechnology research and development, with India and China becoming key players in the production and distribution of vaccines globally.

- **Genomics:** Research in genomics and genetic medicine is growing, with the creation of gene banks and large-scale sequencing projects.

K. Artificial Intelligence and Automation

BRICS have recognized artificial intelligence (AI) and automation as key sectors for future economic growth and global competitiveness.

- **AI Adoption:** China positions itself as a global leader in AI adoption and development, with the goal of becoming the world's primary hub for AI innovation by 2030.

- **Ethics and AI:** There are growing discussions about the ethical implications of AI and the policies needed to ensure ethically acceptable and socially beneficial development and adoption of AI.

L. Cybersecurity

In an era of growing digitization, cybersecurity becomes essential.

- **Cyber Attacks:** With the increase in cyber threats, BRICS are actively engaged in developing advanced cybersecurity solutions and training experts in the field.

- **Cybersecurity Policies:** The establishment of robust policies and protocols to ensure the security of critical infrastructure and user data is crucial.

M. Space and Satellite Technology

Space technology is another area in which BRICS countries are striving to make significant advancements.

- **Space Missions:** China and India have successfully launched various space missions, with objectives ranging from lunar exploration to satellite launches for climate monitoring.

- **Space Cooperation:** Cooperation within the BRICS bloc can involve sharing resources and knowledge in the field of space technology.

N. Education and Technological Training

For sustainable growth in the technology sector, a solid investment in education is indispensable.

- **STEM Education:** A strong emphasis on Science, Technology, Engineering, and Mathematics (STEM) education is crucial for developing talents that can drive future innovation.

- **Universities and Research:** Universities in BRICS countries are becoming increasingly recognized for research in advanced technological fields.

O. Regulatory Policies and Law

Technological innovation also requires an adequate regulatory framework to support and guide the safe development of new technologies.

- **Intellectual Property:** Issues related to intellectual property and patents are essential for protecting innovations and encouraging further research and development.

- **AI Regulations:** AI regulation, including privacy and data usage issues, is an area that requires attention and development by BRICS countries.

P. Agritech and Agricultural Innovation

Technological innovation is not limited to urban centers or traditional IT sectors but also has a significant impact on agriculture.

- **Agricultural Technologies:** New technologies, including drones, IoT, and robotics, are finding innovative applications in agriculture, with a particular focus on sustainability and efficiency.

- **Bioengineering:** Research in the agricultural field ranges from creating new crop varieties to producing food more efficiently and sustainably.

Each of these points represents a vital sector and facet of innovation and technological development within BRICS nations. Development trajectories, goals, and challenges vary among members; however, they share a common interest in cultivating technological advancements and maintaining a prominent position on the global stage of innovation. As the global technological landscape continues to evolve, BRICS are likely to remain key agents in shaping the future of global technological innovation, with each country having its own specializations and areas of excellence.

Q. Biotechnologies and Healthcare

The challenge of global health and the advancement of biotechnologies are fundamental areas for BRICS nations.

- **Vaccine Development:** During the COVID-19 pandemic, countries like Russia and India played significant roles in the development and production of vaccines, demonstrating significant expertise in biotechnologies and pharmaceutical manufacturing.

- **Genetic Research:** Innovation in genetics and gene therapies has become fundamental areas of research and development, with applications ranging from the treatment of genetic diseases to the development of new pharmacological therapies.

R. Smart Cities and Urbanization

With growing urbanization, BRICS are developing infrastructures and technologies for smarter and more sustainable cities.

- **Smart Infrastructures:** The construction of intelligent urban infrastructures, from connected street lighting to efficient transportation systems, is a priority.

- **Urban Security:** The application of technologies such as facial recognition and intelligent traffic monitoring systems contributes to urban safety and efficient management of metropolises.

S. Industry 4.0 and Manufacturing

BRICS play a pivotal role in the evolution towards Industry 4.0.

- **Robotics:** Robotics applied to industrial production is crucial for increasing efficiency, reducing costs, and improving production quality.

- **Interconnectivity:** Production systems are increasingly interconnected and intelligent, utilizing the Internet of Things (IoT) and other digital technologies to optimize processes.

T. E-commerce and Digitalization

The expansion of e-commerce and the digitization of retail are evident phenomena in BRICS countries.

- **Digital Platforms:** E-commerce is growing exponentially, and platforms like Alibaba (China) have become global giants in online retail.

- **Digital Payments:** The adoption of digital and cryptographic payment systems is reshaping the financial and retail landscape in BRICS countries.

U. Environment and Green Technologies

Environmental sustainability through technological innovation is another key area of interest and development.

- **Renewable Energies:** Investment and development in renewable energy technologies, such as solar and wind power, are essential for a sustainable energy future.

- **Decarbonization Technologies:** Technologies contributing to the decarbonization of various industrial sectors, including CCS (Carbon Capture and Storage) and circular economy solutions, are gaining ground.

Technology and innovation in BRICS nations encompass an incredibly wide range of sectors and applications. In each area, these countries are exploring and implementing solutions to address both national and global challenges, often through a mix of private and public initiatives. The vastness and depth of innovation and technological development within BRICS are extraordinary and will continue to shape the global future of technological innovation in significant and sometimes unforeseen ways. Collaboration among these countries could also accelerate the development and adoption of new technologies, creating new opportunities and perhaps new challenges along the way.

V. Artificial Intelligence and Big Data

BRICS are also focusing on the development of Artificial Intelligence (AI) and Big Data technologies, considering the transformative impact of these technologies on various sectors.

- **AI in Industry:** In China, AI has been extensively employed in manufacturing to optimize processes and improve product quality through continuous monitoring and data analysis.

- **Recommendation Systems:** In e-commerce, AI-based recommendation systems are used to personalize the shopping experience by analyzing user data and predicting their preferences.

W. Space and Aerospace Technology

BRICS have significant ambitions in aerospace technology development and space exploration.

- **Space Missions:** China has launched space missions for lunar and Mars exploration, while India has gained recognition for its cost-effective space missions.

- **Satellites:** The launch and use of satellites for communication, meteorology, and Earth observation are crucial aspects of these nations' space policies.

X. Cybersecurity and Data Protection

Increasing digitization has made cybersecurity and data protection top priorities for BRICS nations.

- **Critical Infrastructure Security:** Ensuring that critical infrastructures are protected from cyberattacks is vital for national security and each BRICS nation's economy.

- **Personal Data Protection:** Data protection and user privacy have become central, with countries like India and Brazil implementing regulations to safeguard citizens' information.

Y. Nanotechnology and Advanced Materials

Research and development in the field of nanotechnologies and advanced materials offer huge potential in various sectors.

- **Medicine:** Nanotechnologies find innovative applications in the medical field, such as targeted therapies and drug delivery.

- **Electronics:** Advanced materials, such as next-generation semiconductors, are driving innovation in electronics and smart devices.

Z. Oceanography and Marine Technologies

Exploration and sustainable utilization of the oceans are vital for future development, considering the vast resources available in terms of biodiversity and minerals.

- **Marine Energy:** Research into technologies to harness tidal and wave energy is of particular interest for a more sustainable energy future.

- **Marine Biology:** Marine biotechnology, exploring the use of marine organisms to develop new drugs and materials, is a growing sector.

BRICS nations, through a combination of state initiatives, international collaborations, and industry-driven innovations, are progressively expanding their impact and influence in advanced technologies and innovation. The growing expansion across various technology fields promises to reshape the global balance of technological power and could revolutionize how technology is created, shared, and implemented globally. In any case, the ongoing challenge will be to balance innovation with emerging ethical, legal, and social considerations in these evolving spaces.

BRICS nations have indeed focused on a wide range of technology and innovation sectors to remain competitive on a global scale, further developing various aspects of technologies and promoting research and innovation in many areas.

AA. Environmental Technologies and Sustainability

- **Renewable Energies:** BRICS are heavily investing in renewable energies. China, for example, is one of the world's largest producers of solar panels. India, on the other hand, is seeking to expand its capacity in wind and solar energy, aiming to become a key player in renewable energy.

BB. Biotechnology

- **Genetic Engineering:** Biotechnology is a key area of development for BRICS. Genetic engineering and CRISPR technologies are used in fields such as agriculture to develop genetically modified crops resistant to pests and diseases, and in medicine for gene and personalized therapy research.

- **Biopharmaceuticals:** The biopharmaceutical sector in BRICS is experiencing rapid growth, with increased investments in research and development for the production of vaccines, innovative therapies, and biotechnological pharmaceutical products.

CC. Education and Technological Training

- **STEM Education:** Education in the fields of science, technology, engineering, and mathematics (STEM) is considered fundamental to fuel the future workforce of BRICS and support their innovative and technological ambitions.

- **Professional Training:** There is also an emphasis on professional training and skill development needed to operate in technologically advanced and industrial sectors.

DD. Robotics and Automation

- **Industrial Robotics:** BRICS are expanding the use of robotics in manufacturing and industrial sectors, automating processes, and implementing intelligent robots in various production and logistics lines.

- **Medical Robotics:** The medical sector is experimenting with the introduction of robotic technologies, such as surgical robots that assist doctors during surgeries or automated patient assistance systems.

EE. Internet of Things (IoT)

- **Smart Cities:** IoT plays a central role in the development of smart cities in BRICS nations, where connected sensors and devices are used to enhance the efficiency of urban services and the quality of life for citizens.

- **Industry 4.0:** IoT is also a fundamental component of Industry 4.0, connecting machinery and industrial devices, enabling more efficient equipment management and maintenance.

As BRICS nations continue to explore and develop their capabilities in these aforementioned sectors, it is evident that the geopolitical context, international collaborations, trade agreements, and global technological advancements will have a significant impact on how these nations navigate and shape the future of their technological and innovative landscape.

Collaboration among BRICS nations, together with careful consideration of the ethical and social implications of emerging technologies, will continue to be vital in supporting and guiding sustainable and inclusive development in the context of a globalized and interconnected society. Striking a balance between growth, innovation, sustainability, and inclusivity will be a fundamental challenge in the coming years, with BRICS exploring various strategies to achieve a fair and resilient transition into the future.

Conclusion: Technology and Innovation in BRICS

Global Incubators of Innovation

BRICS nations, through continuous investment and commitment in various technology and innovation fields, are shaping up as propelling forces in the global technology landscape. These countries have demonstrated specific interest and strategic implementation in emerging technology areas, dedicating significant resources to become leaders in various sectors, as highlighted by several examples in fields such as green technologies, biotechnology, and robotics.

Addressing Disparities

While BRICS nations are advancing, there is an imperative need to address existing disparities at both national and international levels. The divide between urban and rural areas in terms of technology access, as well as differences in innovation capabilities among BRICS nations, are issues that require attention and action. Therefore, inclusive policies and coordinated efforts are crucial to ensure that the benefits of technology and innovation are distributed equitably across all spheres of society.

Collaborations and Partnerships

Partnerships, both domestically and internationally, are critical to BRICS' success in the technology field. Working with various entities, such as businesses, universities, research institutions, and other countries, is essential to expand the pool of knowledge and expertise. Collaborations can also facilitate technology sharing, engagement in joint research projects, and access to global markets, all of which can amplify innovation and BRICS' competitiveness on the world stage.

Ethical and Regulatory Challenges

The ethical and regulatory implications of new technologies must be carefully examined and navigated by BRICS nations. Issues such as privacy, data security, and the socio-economic implications of emerging technologies need to be addressed through robust regulations, public dialogue, and, when necessary, international collaborations to establish global standards.

Toward a Sustainable and Innovative Future

Finally, looking to the future, BRICS, with their substantial innovation and growth potential, have the responsibility and opportunity to lead the world toward a more sustainable and technologically advanced future. Commitment to creating technologies that not only drive economic growth but also address critical issues such as climate change, inequality, and security is essential. This will require a balanced and multidimensional approach that prioritizes sustainability, equity, and resilience, ensuring that technological innovations benefit not only the economies of BRICS but society as a whole.

In summary, technology and innovation in BRICS nations are not only engines of economic growth and development but also a means through which these countries can realize and contribute to common global goals, creating a future where technology is a shared, accessible, and beneficial asset for all.

8. Sustainable Development

Sustainable Development in BRICS

The BRICS nations (Brazil, Russia, India, China, and South Africa) play a critical role in shaping the world towards a path of sustainable development. Each of these nations possesses significant resources and populations, implying that their sustainability policies and practices have a considerable global impact.

Brazil: Biodiversity and Renewable Energy

Brazil, with its vast biodiversity and extensive ecosystems, has placed emphasis on biodiversity conservation and sustainable resource use. There has also been a focus on promoting renewable energy, especially hydroelectric power and biofuel production, while simultaneously addressing challenges related to deforestation and protecting indigenous lands.

Russia: Natural Resource Management and Conservation

Russia, with its vast reserves of natural gas and oil, faces challenges in balancing the exploitation of these resources with environmental preservation. Attention to the conservation of its extensive wilderness and sustainable management of its natural resources is crucial in its sustainable development policies.

India: Inclusive Growth and Green Solutions

India has focused on inclusive growth, aiming to balance rapid economic development with the need for equity and sustainability. The promotion of green technologies, improvement of energy efficiency, and poverty reduction are some of the key goals of its sustainable development policies.

China: Green Industrialization and Innovation

China has explored paths to green industrialization, focusing on clean technologies and sustainable production practices to reduce the environmental impact of its massive industrial output. Innovation in environmental technologies and the development of eco-friendly cities are integral to its sustainability strategy.

South Africa: Inequality Reduction and Environmental Protection

South Africa has placed an emphasis on reducing inequalities and protecting the environment. Balancing industrialization with the protection of its rich biodiversity and ecosystems is a crucial element of its policies.

Collaborations and Common Challenges

While BRICS nations have distinct paths to sustainable development, they share common challenges and have initiated collaborations through various forums and platforms. This includes dialogue on issues such as climate change, natural resource management, and the promotion of clean energy. Cooperation and knowledge sharing among these nations are essential to drive collective actions and support individual efforts towards sustainability.

Final Considerations

As emerging powers, BRICS nations have the opportunity and responsibility to shape a development path that not only meets the immediate needs of their citizens but also safeguards the future of the planet. The policies and practices adopted by these nations will significantly influence the world's ability to achieve the United Nations Sustainable Development Goals (SDGs) and navigate towards a fairer and more sustainable future. The integration of economic, social, and environmental strategies, through national policies and international collaborations, will be crucial in defining BRICS' success in sustainable development.

The theme of sustainable development in BRICS nations remains particularly relevant in the global context, considering the enormous impact these countries have on the international stage in economic, social, and environmental terms. While an overview of how each nation addresses this theme has already been outlined, it is possible to delve further by exploring various sub-aspects and facets.

The challenges related to sustainable development for BRICS nations are incredibly diverse, stemming from the unique geographical, cultural, economic, and social contexts of each. For example, each of the BRICS nations has a different demographic and socio-economic profile that influences consumption patterns, energy and resource demand, and the ability to mitigate and adapt to climate change.

At the same time, the BRICS are also among the leading contributors to global greenhouse gas emissions, with China and India among the top emitters worldwide. The implication of this on the need to develop and implement sustainable technologies and practices is enormous, both at the national level and for their global impact.

It is also interesting to explore how sustainable development policies are influenced and, in turn, influence domestic and external political dynamics. The need to ensure energy security, for instance, can push investments in renewable energies but also in fossil fuel-based solutions.

The dilemma between promoting economic growth and protecting the environment is a persistent tension in sustainable development policies. Efforts to stimulate the economy often clash with sustainability goals, and finding a balance between these two needs requires political skill and willingness.

On the other hand, environmental sustainability can also offer economic opportunities. For example, the renewable energy industry, including solar, wind, and other renewable sources, has the potential to create jobs and stimulate economic growth while simultaneously addressing the climate crisis.

Urbanization patterns and the expansion of cities in BRICS nations represent another crucial area for sustainable development. Rapid and often unplanned urbanization can lead to significant challenges in waste management, air and water pollution, and other environmental issues. At the same time, cities are drivers of innovation and economic development, and their role in shaping a sustainable future cannot be underestimated.

In the global context, BRICS nations play a key role in defining the sustainable development agenda, influencing not only the development trajectories of their own countries but also international dynamics related to climate change, biodiversity, and other key environmental issues. Therefore, the intersection between national policies and actions at the international level becomes a relevant area to explore further.

The analysis of the policies, programs, and specific initiatives that have been implemented in BRICS nations to promote sustainable development can provide insights into how lessons learned and best practices can be shared and adapted in different national and regional contexts. This, in turn, can enrich the discussion and practice of global sustainable development, contributing to shaping a future that balances the needs of the economy, society, and the environment in an equitable and resilient manner. This analysis can be further deepened, exploring various aspects and facets of each practice and policy, all within the context of a holistic and integrated vision of sustainable development.

Digging deeper into the theme of sustainable development among BRICS nations, let's explore how each nation manages the dilemma between economic development and environmental protection through the use of different strategies and methods.

For example, the BRICS countries are progressively increasing their investments in renewable energy. China, for instance, has become one of the world's leading producers and consumers of solar energy, while India has launched ambitious wind and solar energy projects to reduce dependence on fossil fuels. Russia, with vast energy resources, is gradually implementing policies to diversify energy sources and integrate renewable energy into the national energy mix. These investments are motivated not only by the need to reduce greenhouse gas emissions but also by the desire to support economic growth through the development of new industrial sectors.

Sustainable infrastructure is another key area where BRICS nations are striving to reconcile development and sustainability. This involves creating more sustainable cities through urban planning, constructing energy-efficient buildings, and developing low-carbon public transportation systems. This represents an opportunity both to improve the quality of life for citizens and to stimulate innovation and job creation.

Sustainability in supply chains is another fundamental aspect that BRICS nations are exploring. Promoting sustainable agricultural practices, responsible natural resource management, and the implementation of strategies for responsible production and consumption are crucial to ensure that economic development does not come at the expense of the environment and local communities.

Moreover, BRICS nations are developing various policies and financial instruments to support the transition to a greener and more resilient economy. This includes using tax incentives to stimulate investments in sustainable sectors, creating funds to support environmental conservation projects, and promoting socially responsible investment.

In a long-term perspective, education and training play a fundamental role in promoting sustainability within BRICS nations. Integrating sustainability into curricula, promoting research and innovation in fields related to sustainable development, and building capacity and skills in the labor market to support the transition to greener sectors are all strategies being pursued.

Equitable and sustainable access to resources, especially water and energy, poses a significant challenge in BRICS nations characterized by huge socio-economic inequalities. Creating systems that ensure universal access to essential services and resources in a sustainable and equitable manner is essential to ensure that sustainable development benefits all citizens.

At the same time, BRICS countries are actively engaged in international forums related to sustainable development, such as the United Nations' Agenda 2030 and the Paris Agreement on climate change. In these contexts, they act both as representatives of their own national interests and as influential voices for developing countries in general.

Lastly, issues of governance, transparency, and public participation are also vital when it comes to sustainable development in the BRICS. The participation of all stakeholders, including the private sector, civil society, and local communities, is essential to create sustainable and inclusive solutions rooted in the needs and aspirations of the people.

These reflections represent only some of the many facets of sustainable development in BRICS nations, and one could continue to delve into each of these aspects through detailed and specific analysis, assessing the policies, strategies, and initiatives implemented, as well as the challenges and opportunities that arise in each national and regional context.

In conclusion, the policies and practices of sustainable development adopted by BRICS nations are a fundamental part of the mosaic of their economic and social development, as they simultaneously address environmental, economic, and social issues. On one hand, the main challenge for these countries is to balance the urgent need for socioeconomic development, including industrialization, urbanization, and economic growth, with environmental protection and responsible use of natural resources.

The BRICS, with their growing economies and populations, have a significant impact on global climate and the environment, but they are also experiencing firsthand the effects of climate change and environmental degradation. For example, issues related to air quality, water resource management, and biodiversity loss are just some of the critical issues they must address, requiring ingenious and sustainable solutions.

While each BRICS nation faces unique challenges in terms of sustainable development, they all share a common aspiration to promote development that not only meets current needs but also ensures the stability and prosperity of future generations. In this context, the concept of sustainable development is translated into national policies and implementation strategies that seek to balance sometimes conflicting objectives while ensuring a fair distribution of development opportunities and benefits.

The efforts made by BRICS countries to promote sustainable development through energy transition, technological innovation, sustainable natural resource management, and the promotion of social equity are particularly relevant in the global context. Their initiatives not only influence development trajectories within their borders but also shape global environmental governance and sustainable development.

Another aspect that emerges is the importance of cooperation at both intraregional and international levels. Cooperation among BRICS countries, as well as between BRICS and other nations and regions, is essential for sharing knowledge, experiences, and best practices regarding sustainable development. This mutual exchange not only strengthens each nation's capacity to pursue sustainable development goals but also promotes the construction of a fairer and more sustainable international order.

In conclusion, the path taken by BRICS nations to ensure sustainable development will require ongoing commitment, well-thought-out strategies, and strong political will. The role of BRICS in the global landscape, their internal challenges and opportunities, and the interconnectedness between sustainable development issues and other areas such as security, technology, and health make their management of sustainable development policies and practices a globally relevant topic that will undoubtedly influence the economic, social, and environmental dynamics of the 21st century.

9. Inequalities and Disparities

The examination of inequalities and disparities within and among BRICS countries (Brazil, Russia, India, China, and South Africa) is a critical issue that intersects various aspects of social, economic, and political development. Despite significant economic progress in recent decades, these countries face substantial challenges related to internal inequalities and disparities among them.

Internal Inequalities:

1. **Economic:** There is a visible income and wealth disparity within these countries. Wealth distribution is heavily skewed, with wealthy minorities holding a significant share of national resources.

2. **Social:** Social inequalities manifest in various ways, such as limited access to healthcare, education, and other essential resources and opportunities for certain segments of the population.

3. **Gender:** In several BRICS countries, women and girls face substantial inequalities in terms of access to education, employment opportunities, political representation, and control over resources.

4. **Ethnic and Cultural:** Significant disparities exist among different ethnic and cultural groups, affecting both economic opportunities and access to rights and opportunities.

Disparities Among BRICS Countries:

1. **Economic Development:** Despite all being considered emerging economies, there are significant differences in terms of GDP, the size

of the economy, and production capacity among BRICS countries.

2. **Political Structures:** Each BRICS country has a distinct political and governmental structure, resulting in different response capabilities and approaches to inequality issues.

3. **Social Policies:** There are substantial differences in social policies, including welfare systems and social protection.

4. **Environmental Management:** BRICS countries exhibit a variety of approaches and capabilities in managing environmental issues and climate challenges.

Examples: India faces enormous challenges related to caste and religious inequalities, while Brazil grapples with economic disparities and violence. Russia confronts growing economic inequalities and wealth concentration among a narrow elite. China has significant regional disparities in economic development between coastal and inland areas. South Africa, on the other hand, has one of the highest income inequalities globally, stemming from both historical factors and current challenges.

Inter-country Perspective: In terms of inter-country perspective, China dominates in terms of economic size and global influence, while countries like

South Africa face more pronounced challenges regarding economic stability and growth. India stands out for its demographics and the scale of its development challenges. Russia plays a key geopolitical role but faces economic and demographic issues. Brazil, plagued by political instability and social problems, continues its struggle for social justice and economic stability.

Addressing these inequalities and disparities requires a joint focus on equitable domestic policies and international cooperation and solidarity. BRICS countries can learn from each other and support each other on the path towards more inclusive and sustainable development.

Within the discourse on inequalities and disparities in BRICS countries, it is essential to explore in-depth the socio-cultural matrix, demographic dynamics, future prospects, and the geopolitics of each nation and the block as a whole.

Demographic Dynamics and Future Prospects: Demographics play a fundamental role in disparities among BRICS countries. In India, for example, a young population with a high percentage lacking access to quality education and healthcare poses a significant challenge to realizing its demographic potential. Conversely, China is grappling with an aging population, which could impact its economic growth and social sustainability. Brazil and South Africa face different demographic pressures, needing to create opportunities for a young and growing workforce. Russia, with a demographic leaning towards an aging population and a decreasing working-age population, has its unique challenges in terms of development sustainability.

Geopolitics and Foreign Influences: The geopolitical position and history of each BRICS country greatly influence their development trajectories and related inequalities. For example, economic sanctions imposed on Russia have had an impact on various sectors of its economic and social systems. China is currently at the center of numerous geopolitical tensions, and how these might affect its economy and society is a critical issue. India, situated in a region with various cross-border tensions, must balance its development priorities with strategic and security needs.

Emerging Global Challenges: Emerging global challenges such as climate change, pandemics, and digitalization pose new questions about inequalities. For example, while digitalization offers opportunities for economic and social development, it can also exacerbate existing inequalities, both within countries and among them. The global health crisis associated with COVID-19 has revealed and intensified existing disparities, exposing the vulnerabilities of healthcare systems and social safety nets.

Policies and International Cooperation

The creation of policies specifically aimed at reducing inequalities is essential. This includes policies targeting income disparity, improving access to education and healthcare, and promoting gender equality. Additionally, while each BRICS country has its unique matrix of inequality, there are lessons and practices that can be shared among them, creating a framework for South-South cooperation.

Urban and Rural Development

Disparity in urban and rural development is another critical factor when exploring inequalities. While some urban areas within BRICS countries enjoy rapid development and modernization, many rural areas lag behind, creating a gap in well-being and opportunities available to people in these diverse regions.

Challenges are multiple and complex and require sophisticated strategies and well-considered policies, as well as effective multilateral cooperation to be effectively addressed. In this context, cooperation among BRICS countries, as well as with other global partners, can play a significant role in sharing

knowledge, expertise, and resources to tackle the persistent and emerging challenges of inequalities and disparities.

Investments and Capital Flows

The analysis of inequalities and disparities in BRICS countries cannot ignore an assessment of investments and capital flows. Foreign Direct Investments (FDI) and capital flows within BRICS countries highlight significant inequalities. Some regions and sectors attract substantial investments, while others are neglected, contributing to the creation and perpetuation of disparities. For example, China has attracted significant FDI, becoming a global hub for manufacturing. However, this has also caused severe regional disparities, with coastal areas thriving much more than inland regions.

Fiscal Policies and Inequalities

Fiscal policies, how governments collect and spend resources, play a fundamental role in determining the levels of inequality within a country. For example, in Brazil, despite a series of social policies, inequalities remain highly visible due to persistent injustices in the tax system and spending structures, which often benefit elites rather than the most vulnerable social groups.

Educational Systems and Disparities

Access to and quality of education are other crucial aspects of inequalities within and among BRICS countries. In India, for example, access to higher education is highly polarized along socio-economic and geographic lines, contributing to perpetuating intergenerational cycles of poverty and inequality. Education policies that fail to reach the most disadvantaged segments of society contribute to creating an inequality cycle that is difficult to break.

Gender Disparities and Social Inclusion

Gender inequality is a pressing issue in BRICS countries. Despite progress, women in BRICS countries often face substantial barriers in terms of access to employment, wage parity, and representation in leadership positions. South Africa, for example, has actively worked to improve gender equality through various laws and initiatives, but significant challenges related to structural and cultural issues persist.

Regional Integration and Connectivity

Regional integration and connectivity between different parts of BRICS countries show disparities in terms of development and opportunities. In vast nations like Russia, regional inequality is significant, and equity in access to opportunities, services, and infrastructure among different regions remains a persistent issue fueling socio-economic disparities.

Environmental Policies and Sustainable Development

The approach to sustainable development and environmental policies within BRICS countries reflects another spectrum of inequalities. Countries like China have experienced significant environmental degradation as a direct result of rapid industrialization, disproportionately impacting vulnerable populations that often live in areas with high levels of pollution.

Social Mobility and Labor

Social mobility, the ability of individuals to improve their socio-economic status, is closely tied to job opportunities and education. In BRICS countries, social mobility varies significantly, and in some cases, such as Brazil, significant barriers prevent people from advancing economically and socially, reinforcing cycles of poverty and inequality. The issue of wealth distribution and access to opportunities becomes central, and policies to address the growing gap between the rich and the poor are indispensable for a sustainable and equitable future.

Conflicts and Inequalities

The presence of conflicts, both internal and with neighboring nations, heavily influences inequalities within BRICS countries. For example, in India, prolonged conflict in regions like Jammu and Kashmir has fueled disparities and inequalities not only at the regional level but has also influenced national policies and priorities.

Preliminary Conclusions

While each BRICS country faces its unique challenges in terms of inequalities and disparities, there are common and shared themes that emerge across the bloc, including regional disparities, gender inequality, and inequalities in access to fundamental services such as education and healthcare. These elements are essential for developing a holistic understanding of inequalities and disparities in the BRICS and require further analysis and detailed consideration in political and academic discourse.

Inequalities and Disparities in BRICS Countries: Conclusion

BRICS countries, despite sharing some growth and development trends, exhibit considerable complexity in terms of social, economic, and environmental inequalities and disparities. The realities of Brazil, Russia, India, China, and South Africa intersect and diverge on multiple levels, spanning socio-economic, gender, environmental, and regional integration spheres.

Socio-economic Inequalities and Social Mobility

Socio-economic inequalities in BRICS countries are intertwined with social mobility. Structural barriers to education, access to qualified job opportunities, and quality healthcare hinder social mobility, keeping existing disparities unchanged. The consolidation of an economic elite at the expense of impoverished masses further exacerbates these inequalities. The issue of wealth distribution and access to opportunities becomes central, and policies to counter the widening gap between the rich and the poor are indispensable for a sustainable and equitable future.

Gender and Disparities

Gender inequality continues to permeate BRICS societies despite political and social efforts. Gender discrimination manifests in areas such as pay, employment, education, and political representation. Addressing these issues is not only imperative from a human rights perspective but is also essential for socioeconomic progress, as women's empowerment is closely linked to sustainable development.

Regional Disparities

Regional disparities, especially in vast countries like Russia and China, are significant. Central and coastal regions, often more developed, contrast with inner and peripheral areas struggling with inadequate infrastructure, limited opportunities, and development challenges. These geographical inequalities require targeted strategies to balance development and ensure that resources and opportunities are distributed more evenly.

Environment and Sustainable Development

The dialogue between development and environmental protection intersects with inequalities, where often the poorest communities bear the brunt of environmental degradation. The environmental policies of BRICS countries must, therefore, consider how sustainability strategies can be inclusive and not generate further disparities.

Tools and Strategies for Change

In order to reverse the trajectory of inequalities and disparities in BRICS countries, the creation and implementation of inclusive policies become fundamental. This requires a combination of proactive fiscal policies, investments in education and health, regional development strategies, and gender empowerment programs. Additionally, ongoing dialogue among BRICS countries to share knowledge and best practices could serve as a catalyst for developing innovative and collaborative solutions to address these common challenges.

Towards a Fairer and More Sustainable Future

The path toward a fairer future for BRICS countries is undeniably challenging and requires concerted commitment from governments, the private sector, and civil society. Addressing inequalities and disparities involves building a more resilient and integrated social and economic fabric, where the benefits of development are shared more widely, and where every citizen has the opportunity to realize their potential.

In this perspective, the lessons learned from each BRICS country should illuminate the way toward more inclusive and just strategies, ensuring that future development is not only economically robust but also equitably distributed across all sectors of society.

10. Conflicts and Cooperation • Analysis of conflicts and areas of cooperation among BRICS members.

Conflicts and Cooperation among BRICS Members

1. Overview

The BRICS countries (Brazil, Russia, India, China, and South Africa) have represented a significant entity in global politics and economics. Although united by common interests such as economic development and reform of international financial institutions, they manifest a range of divergences and conflicts coexisting with areas of cooperation.

2. Evident Conflicts among BRICS Members

a. Economic and Trade Divergences China and India have experienced trade tensions related to imbalances in trade and tariff barriers. Brazil has also expressed concerns about Chinese trade practices and competition in the agricultural sector.

b. Territorial Conflicts The most prominent territorial conflict within BRICS is between India and China, especially along their vast mountainous border, with historical disputes and recent military skirmishes.

c. Ideological and Political Divergences Political and ideological differences among members, such as the parliamentary democracy of India contrasting with China's more centralized system, have generated frictions and misalignments in foreign and domestic policies.

3. Areas of Cooperation

a. Economic Cooperation Despite conflicts, BRICS members have identified and pursued areas of economic collaboration, such as the New Development Bank, established to finance sustainable and infrastructural development projects in BRICS countries and other emerging economies.

b. Security and Politics BRICS work jointly on security and political issues in some international forums, seeking to consolidate their weight and influence in the international system and advocating for the reform of global institutions such as the IMF and the World Bank.

c. Cultural and Educational Exchange The countries have promoted initiatives to intensify cultural and educational exchanges, aiming to build bridges and promote mutual understanding among the peoples of BRICS.

4. A Delicate Balance between Conflict and Cooperation

The relationship among BRICS countries is a delicate balance between cooperation and competition. On one hand, there is a common willingness to collaborate in some areas of mutual interest; on the other hand, rivalries and conflicts, both historical and current, represent significant obstacles to fully realizing the group's potential.

Security, trade, and global influence issues are particularly sensitive areas. For instance, the growing global presence of China, both economically and militarily, is viewed with suspicion by other members, especially India, fueling tensions and suspicions.

5. Towards a Future of Increased Collaboration?

The challenge for BRICS in the near future will be to navigate these tumultuous waters, seeking to minimize conflicts and maximize areas of cooperation. This may require compromises, flexibility, and renewed commitment to dialogue and mutual understanding.

Long-Term Perspective

In the long term, the ability of the BRICS to overcome divergences and focus on shared goals and interests will determine the group's success and influence in the global landscape. In an increasingly multipolar and interconnected world, multilateral cooperation among countries with significant resources and influence, such as the BRICS, will be crucial in addressing the global challenges that lie ahead.

The dynamics of conflict and cooperation within the BRICS also intertwine and develop in relation to external influences and global dynamics. The fragmentation and synergies among these emerging states are constantly evolving, reflecting both tensions and common interests that shape their interactions.

For example, the trade war between China and the United States, which reached its peak in 2018-2019, had implications for all BRICS economies. China, in particular, sought to diversify its trading partners and invest in new markets, a move that had competitive and collaborative repercussions for Brazil, Russia, India, and South Africa. While

The digital sphere also emerges as a dynamic field of cooperation and rivalry. For example, China has supported India in developing digital infrastructure through direct investments in startups and emerging technologies. However, concerns regarding national security, data privacy, and intellectual property remain sources of tension between the two countries, tensions that also extend and reverberate in their interactions with Brazil, Russia, and South Africa.

Simultaneously, global energy transition and the commitment to greater sustainability create new dynamics among BRICS members. China, for instance, has made significant commitments to carbon neutrality, while India is heavily investing in solar energy. Russia, while maintaining a prominent role as an exporter of gas and oil, is also exploring possibilities in the field of renewable energy. These developments create cooperative scenarios in which BRICS countries can share technologies and expertise, but also potential conflicts in terms of energy markets, investments, and environmental policies.

Furthermore, the BRICS as entities also seek to establish a counterbalance to Western influence in terms of global economic governance, and to do so, they need to strengthen their internal cohesion by promoting joint dialogues and initiatives, although political and economic divergences remain evident. This often manifests in multilateral forums, where BRICS countries present united fronts on key issues such as institutional reform and the promotion of greater equity in global power distribution.

However, the relationship between BRICS countries cannot be fully understood without also considering the domestic socio-political context of each member. Economic growth, the expansion of the middle class, inequalities, and internal political stability in each nation significantly influence the directions of foreign policies and positions adopted towards other BRICS members and, more broadly, in the international arena.

The future of the BRICS and their impact on the international system will continue to be shaped by a complex matrix of conflicts and cooperation, intersecting areas such as trade, security, technology, and sustainability. It will be essential to monitor how these dynamics evolve in the context of a changing global order and increasingly pressing global challenges.

Balancing Cooperation and Competition

As the BRICS seek to navigate the waters of complex global challenges, they are constantly seeking strategies that can balance cooperation and competitiveness in an ever-evolving international context. Internal rivalry and solidarity within the group emerge not only in economic terms but also regarding security and geopolitics, making their cooperative path both fertile and complex.

One particularly interesting lens through which to further explore these themes is the geopolitics of COVID-19 vaccinations. The pandemic posed an unprecedented challenge to international cooperation and exacerbated and highlighted some of the existing tensions within and among the BRICS. For example, India and South Africa led global efforts to waive patents on COVID-19 vaccines, proposing a waiver to the World Trade Organization (WTO) to facilitate vaccine production in developing countries. This position illuminated not only North-South dynamics in vaccine production and distribution but also emphasized the BRICS' aspiration to shape global norms and practices to be more equitable and favorable to emerging and developing countries.

Furthermore, the growing vaccine nationalism has represented another point of tension, with countries like China and Russia using "vaccine diplomacy" as a tool to expand their influence in key regions such as Africa and Latin America. This raised questions about how BRICS countries can balance national interests with collective ones, especially when it comes to addressing global challenges that require coordinated and solidary responses.

Additionally, the BRICS' path in the international landscape is also influenced by internal cooperation structures within the group. The BRICS New Development Bank (NDB), for example, serves as a crucial tool for financing infrastructure projects within member countries and offering an alternative to Western lending mechanisms. However, the NDB must navigate tensions and divergent interests among its members, seeking to balance the need to finance projects that are both economically sustainable and geopolitically acceptable to all BRICS countries.

Expansion of 5G Technology

The expansion of 5G technologies represents another field of potential cooperation and conflict among BRICS countries. China, through technology giants like Huawei, has made significant advancements in the development and deployment of 5G technology, positioning itself as a global leader. However, concerns related to data security and privacy, particularly from India, highlight how BRICS countries can find themselves both as partners and rivals in the global technology arena.

The intersection of these and many other issues, from cybersecurity to artificial intelligence, from space cooperation to natural resource management, will shape the future trajectory of BRICS in the international context, molding their ability to operate as both cooperative blocs and rival nations, each with its own geopolitical and geo-economic agenda and priorities. Continued exploration of these dynamics is therefore essential for understanding potential future trajectories of international relations and the configuration of global power in the contemporary era.

Exploring Intra-BRICS Relations

To delve further into the nuances of intra-BRICS relations, we might note that the interaction among these states reveals an exciting amalgamation of expectations, aspirations, and caution. While economic relations among these countries often capture global media attention, a less explored but equally crucial aspect is the realm of security and military alliances.

It is significant to note that, although the BRICS represent a united front on numerous global economic and political issues, security cooperation has not followed a parallel path. Regional rivalries, territorial disputes, and differences in alliance and security models have led to a sort of delay in the formulation of a common security front. Take, for example, the complex triangle of relations between China, India, and Russia.

While Russia and India have enjoyed long-standing positive bilateral relations, especially in terms of military cooperation and arms purchases, India-China relations have been marked by tensions, highlighted by territorial disputes and a border war. Similarly, Russia-China relations are complex, blending elements of cooperation and mutual suspicion, despite an outward facade of a strategic alliance.

Managing these complex trilateral relations, within the broader context of BRICS, represents an extremely delicate geopolitical dance. While the bloc has succeeded in articulating a shared vision for a multipolar world order and has worked together in international forums to promote these objectives, building a cohesive framework for security cooperation has remained elusive.

Economic Inequality and Environmental Considerations

Another element deserving special attention is the growing economic inequality within BRICS countries. While these nations have often presented a united front in international forums, emphasizing the need for greater representation and influence for emerging countries, internally they must contend with issues of income and wealth inequality. For example, while China and India have seen a significant number of people lifted out of poverty in recent decades, both countries face significant challenges in terms of income and wealth inequality.

The environmental theme is also fundamental. BRICS nations have been among the largest greenhouse gas emitters and have faced criticism for their environmental policies. However, it is essential to emphasize that these nations are also actively seeking to balance economic growth with environmental sustainability, striving to reconcile their roles as leaders in the global South with the requirements of inclusive and sustainable economic growth. For instance, China has made massive investments in renewable energy and has committed to achieving carbon neutrality by 2060.

In conclusion, while BRICS present themselves as a rising economic bloc, the dynamics within the group, including economic cooperation, strategic rivalry, and geopolitical tensions, remain a rich field for exploration and analysis. The need to balance global aspirations with regional and national challenges continues to drive interactions within the group, offering an intricate and fascinating panorama of contemporary international relations.

Regarding the theme of "Conflicts and Cooperation" among BRICS members, the examination of the intricate fabrics of alliances, challenges, and opportunities within the group raises several crucial questions for the future of the world order. The BRICS, composed of Brazil, Russia, India, China, and South Africa, have created a unique forum that, while characterized by a complex mix of cooperation and conflict, has potentially redefined key dynamics of global politics and economics.

Cooperation among BRICS members has often been emphasized in terms of joint economic initiatives, such as the New Development Bank, and united stances in various multilateral forums. The common agenda of BRICS has typically centered on themes like reforming international financial institutions, promoting a more multipolar world order, and sustainable development. However, while these themes have provided common ground, it is also evident that significant tensions, not always openly declared, exist among the bloc's members.

Bilateral Relations Within BRICS

Bilateral Relations within BRICS Bilateral relations among BRICS members are highly variable. For instance, the Sino-Indian relationship has been tense due to territorial disputes and strategic rivalries in the Indian subcontinent and the Indian Ocean. In contrast, the Sino-Russian relationship has enjoyed relatively strong cooperation, especially in terms of coordination in multilateral forums and joint energy projects. Similarly, while Russia has maintained friendly relations with India, including deep defense cooperation, Brazil and South Africa have sometimes played less central roles in the dynamics of cooperation and conflict within the group.

Challenges and China's Growing Power Another critical challenge within BRICS is managing China's growing power. China's enormous economy, rapid technological development, and increasing military influence are factors that could influence future dynamics within the bloc, especially regarding how other members handle their relationships with Beijing. China, despite being an economic growth engine and a key trading partner for all other BRICS members, is also perceived as a security challenge, especially for India but also for Russia in certain contexts.

Consequently, the future of BRICS may be strongly influenced by its members' ability to navigate these internal complexities and tensions. The sustainability of the bloc as a significant forum for economic and political cooperation will largely depend on the willingness and capacity of its members to manage both internal power asymmetries and the challenges and opportunities arising from the evolution of the world order.

The Role and Responsibility of BRICS in the Context of Climate Change

Active Participation in Global Initiatives The BRICS group, consisting of countries with rapid industrialization and significant economic growth, plays a crucial role in the global context of climate change. The collaboration and actions taken by Brazil, Russia, India, China, and South Africa have a significant impact on the international stage, primarily due to their considerable greenhouse gas emissions, growing economies, and increasing energy needs.

These BRICS nations actively participate in international climate negotiations and in the Conference of the Parties (COP) under the United Nations Framework Convention on Climate Change (UNFCCC). Both collectively and individually, these countries are influential in shaping global policies and shaping climate agreements, such as the 2015 Paris Agreement.

Distinct and Diverse Challenges Each BRICS country faces distinct challenges related to climate change. For example, India and China are among the world's largest greenhouse gas emitters, and while both have taken significant initiatives to increase the use of renewable energies, coal dependence remains a significant issue. On the other hand, Brazil has unique challenges related to deforestation in the Amazon and the sustainable management of its biodiversity.

Investments in Renewable Energies and Green Technologies All BRICS countries have made significant investments in renewable energies and green technologies. India, for instance, has set ambitious goals to expand its solar and wind energy capacity. China, on the other hand, is a global leader in solar panel and wind turbine production, while Brazil has a long history of bioethanol production and has integrated biofuels into its energy matrix.

Political and Economic Divergences Despite cooperation, significant divergences exist among BRICS nations' climate policies. While some countries may prioritize economic growth, others may place a greater emphasis on environmental protection and climate mitigation. These divergences are often linked to unique economic, social, and geopolitical factors for each nation, making cooperation on climate change both an opportunity and a challenge.

Vulnerability and Adaptation to Climate Change
BRICS countries are also highly vulnerable to the impacts of climate change, such as extreme weather events, sea-level rise, and changes in precipitation patterns. The need for adaptation is crucial to ensure that vulnerable populations, critical infrastructure, and vital ecosystems are protected from current and future climate changes.

Conclusion Collectively and individually, BRICS countries hold a significant share of the responsibility and power to shape global responses to climate change. Effectively managing their respective internal challenges and building consensus within the group can amplify the effectiveness of their actions on the world stage. The path to fruitful cooperation will require a balance between national and collective goals, economic growth and environmental protection, and national initiatives and participation in multilateral efforts.

If you would like the text to be further expanded or delve into specific subtopics, please let me know!

12. Defense and Security Strategies • Defense and Security Policies of BRICS in the New World Order.

Defense and Security Policies of BRICS in the New World Order The defense and security policies of BRICS nations are inherently linked to their respective geopolitical positions, strategic objectives, and perceptions of threats in the new world order. While BRICS is a relatively cohesive entity in certain areas, such as economic development and climate change issues, it exhibits significant divergences in its approaches and policies concerning defense and security.

Individual Perspectives on Security Threats and Defense Each BRICS state possesses a distinctive set of threat perceptions and strategic objectives. For example, China largely focuses on the South China Sea, Taiwan, and challenges posed by the United States in the region. Russia concentrates on NATO countries and security issues in Eastern Europe and the Arctic. India has significant security concerns regarding its neighbors, particularly Pakistan and China, while Brazil and South Africa are more focused on regional issues and peace and security at the continental level.

Cooperation Mechanisms within BRICS Through various summits and forums, BRICS seeks to promote dialogue and cooperation in security and defense matters, even though joint actions are often limited by national interest divergences. Members have undertaken initiatives to enhance cooperation in cybersecurity, counterterrorism, and military capabilities development while simultaneously fostering dialogue on security issues through regular meetings of defense and security ministers.

Conflicts of Interest and Bilateral Tensions Significant tensions and conflicts of interest also exist within the bloc. A notable example is the territorial tensions between India and China, which have even led to armed clashes along their disputed borders. Such tensions complicate the establishment of a common and cohesive defense and security policy within the BRICS bloc.

BRICS Members on the Global Stage Each BRICS member seeks to assert its own role and influence on the global stage. Russia and China, in particular, are attempting to challenge the existing world order by promoting their own worldviews and seeking to counterbalance Western influence. India, Brazil, and South Africa, on the other hand, often aim to mediate between a wide range of global interests and coalitions, pursuing a foreign policy that balances relations with both the West and other emerging powers.

The Military and Strategic Dimension BRICS' approach to defense and security is also strongly influenced by their military and strategic capabilities. China and Russia, with substantial armed forces and nuclear arsenals, often adopt a more assertive approach in their respective regions compared to other BRICS members. India, as a nuclear power, also takes a robust approach to defense matters, while Brazil and South Africa tend to emphasize preventive diplomacy, mediation, and peacekeeping missions.

Conclusions The defense and security policies of BRICS in the new world order are a mixture of cooperation and competition, with members seeking to balance the promotion of national interests with the maintenance and development of BRICS as a significant international actor. Diverse threat perceptions, strategic priorities, and geopolitical objectives, along with bilateral tensions and rivalries, make security dialogue and cooperation among BRICS a complex and nuanced dynamic that reflects the complexities and paradoxes of the contemporary world order.

Implications in the New World Order BRICS, collectively and individually, have the capacity to shape the global security landscape, advancing both shared and divergent objectives. For example, while there is a general convergence on themes like multilateralism and reform of global institutions, specific strategies and approaches to achieve these goals can vary significantly among members.

Collaborations with Other Nations and Blocs BRICS'
relationships with other nations and power blocs are
also particularly significant in terms of their impact on
global stability and security. Russia and China, for
instance, have established close bilateral cooperation
on numerous defense and security aspects while
simultaneously developing relations with other nations
through forums and organizations like the Shanghai
Cooperation Organization (SCO). India, while sharing
certain forums with Russia and China, has also
cultivated strong ties with Western nations and other
global democracies, further complicating the internal
dynamics of BRICS.

Arms Industry and Military Strategies The arms
industry and military strategies of BRICS nations are
also crucial aspects. For instance, China has
significantly expanded its presence in the global arms
industry, becoming one of the world's largest arms
exporters and thereby influencing power dynamics in
various regions. At the same time, Russia has sought to
maintain and expand its influence as a leading player
in the global arms market.

If you need further details or additional insights into
specific areas, please feel free to ask!

Nuclear Issues Nuclear issues represent another area where BRICS policies have a significant impact. Russia and China are established nuclear powers, while India, despite possessing nuclear weapons, is not recognized as a nuclear-armed state under the Nuclear Non-Proliferation Treaty (NPT). The differing nuclear positions and strategies of BRICS nations influence not only their bilateral relations but also regional and global security dynamics, strategic stability, and non-proliferation efforts.

Cybersecurity and Cyber Warfare In terms of cybersecurity and cyber warfare, BRICS nations are playing an increasingly relevant role, facing challenges both as victims and perpetrators of malicious activities in the cyber domain. Cyber defense strategies, the use of information and communication technologies (ICT) for defense and security, and offensive capabilities in cyberspace are all areas of growing emphasis and development for BRICS nations.

Global Power Projection The projection of military power and the demonstration of strength through military exercises, deployments, and overseas operations are other ways through which BRICS nations are seeking to assert and shape their roles in the new world order. Engagement in United Nations peacekeeping missions, as well as unilateral or multilateral operations in specific contexts, serves as a means to advance interests, establish credentials, and influence regional and global security.

The complexity and nuances of BRICS defense and security policies in the new world order offer a wide range of areas for further analysis and discussion, providing both opportunities and challenges for cooperation and competition among members and with other global actors.

Utilization of Technology in Defense The incorporation of advanced technology into BRICS' defense programs has had a substantial impact on the nations' ability to project power and influence. The introduction of technologies such as artificial intelligence, drones, and cyber warfare platforms has expanded the operational and strategic capabilities of BRICS while also raising new ethical and strategic questions. Emerging technologies also have the potential to redefine the nature of conflict, increasingly focusing attention on non-traditional domains like cyberspace and outer space.

Territorial Tensions and Defensive Strategies Issues related to territorial tensions and national defense strategies represent another area warranting further exploration. For example, India and China have experienced tensions along their mountainous borders, inevitably influencing regional and global security policies. At the same time, Russia faces its own security challenges related to territorial integrity, whether concerning its Western regions and relations with NATO or its Southern regions and security issues in the Caucasus.

Political Ideologies and Nationalism Political ideologies and nationalism also play a fundamental role in BRICS defense policies. The rising wave of nationalism in each of these countries could reinforce existing defense policies and, simultaneously, potentially encourage greater assertiveness on the global stage. This, in turn, could both promote unity within individual BRICS nations and cause tensions within the group and with other nations.

Economic Implications of Defense Policies The economic implications of defense and security policies are another crucial factor to consider. Investments in armed forces and military modernization can have both benefits and drawbacks for the national economies of BRICS. On one hand, it can stimulate defense-related industries and create employment opportunities, while on the other hand, it may divert valuable resources away from other vital sectors such as education and healthcare.

Internal Military Cooperation Internal military cooperation among BRICS nations represents another noteworthy dimension. Despite various bilateral tensions among members, such as those between India and China, the bloc has sought to consolidate a certain degree of military cooperation. Joint military exercises and security dialogue forums within BRICS are tools through which the bloc aims to navigate and mitigate internal tensions while pursuing common security objectives.

Geopolitical Rivalries with Other Blocs

Geopolitical rivalries and power dynamics with other blocs and nations outside of BRICS are a persistent reality that inevitably impacts the group's defense and security policies. BRICS' relationship with nations and groups like the United States, the European Union, and NATO is complex and multifaceted, characterized by a mix of cooperation in certain areas and competition and contention in others.

International Norms and International Law

Finally, the adherence to and interpretation of international norms and international law represent another key element. BRICS defense policies and their impact on the new world order are also contingent on their willingness to conform to, challenge, or redefine existing international norms and legal structures, in areas ranging from disarmament to maritime law.

Each of these elements provides a penetrating view into the complex landscape of BRICS defense and security policies and their implications for the contemporary world order. However, it is crucial to emphasize that the continuously evolving nature of geopolitical dynamics and international relations necessitates ongoing examination and reassessment of these strategies and policies.

Asymmetric Conflicts and New Threats In the current context, we are facing asymmetric threats and conflicts, such as terrorism, cyber warfare, and bio-threats, which require a reevaluation of traditional defense and security structures. For example, cyberattacks have the potential to compromise critical infrastructure, disrupt national economies, and threaten national security. Cyber warfare and disinformation have become increasingly predominant tools in the strategic arsenal of nations, aiming to destabilize societies and politicize internal divisions.

Cybersecurity and Cyber Warfare As emerging powers, the BRICS are actively venturing into the development of their capabilities in the cyber domain, seeking not only to defend against threats but also to craft tools that can be used for defensive and offensive purposes. The integration of technology into their military and security apparatus reflects not only an adaptation to modern threats but also an aspiration to exercise greater control and influence in the global cyberspace domain.

Arms Race and Disarmament Tensions are palpable in terms of the arms race and disarmament policies as well. The BRICS themselves are immersed in a web of complex relationships involving both arms racing and disarmament efforts. The nuclear arsenals of India, Russia, and China and their respective deterrence policies, as well as the proliferation of advanced military technologies, are all issues that need to be examined through a lens that considers both internal dynamics within the BRICS and their relations with other nations.

Social Implications of Defense Policies The social implications of defense and security policies are also noteworthy. Militarization, defense spending, and the increasing emphasis on security can have repercussions on civil rights, resource distribution, and development priorities. Furthermore, the strengthening of military and security structures in each of the BRICS nations can have different implications for human rights, freedom of expression, and the management of protests and internal dissent.

BRICS Relations and Old Powers Additionally, how the BRICS interact with "old powers," namely the United States and European countries, as well as their policies towards strategically important nations like Iran, North Korea, and Pakistan, indicates the direction in which the new world order may evolve. While seeking to reaffirm and solidify their influence and presence in various regions, they are simultaneously engaged in a form of power balancing with the United States and Europe, oscillating between cooperation and confrontation.

Regional Security Policies From a regional security perspective, each of the BRICS nations is involved in a series of conflicts and tensions that require a combination of diplomatic, military, and security approaches to manage and mitigate. For example, Russia's involvement in Ukraine and Syria, India's engagements in its regional neighbors and cross-border conflicts, and China's activities in the South China Sea represent significant challenges that shape their respective security policies and also influence the dynamics within the BRICS bloc.

Conclusion The issue of BRICS defense and security policies cannot be addressed without a deep understanding of the specific challenges that each member faces at the national and international levels. While sharing certain aspirations and objectives with other bloc members, each nation navigates through a unique set of challenges and opportunities that reflect their particular geopolitical, historical, and socio-economic circumstances.

Nonetheless, dialogue and cooperation in terms of defense and security within the BRICS bloc will remain central to their individual and collective strategies, aiming to reaffirm their role and influence in the new world order, and potentially rewriting some of the rules and norms governing international relations and global security. Ultimately, a thorough analysis of BRICS defense and security strategies requires ongoing commitment to understand and interpret the ongoing shifts in the global geopolitical and security landscape, which are in a perpetual state of flux.

Conclusion: BRICS in the Global Defense and Security Discourse The emerging profile of BRICS on the international stage, anchored in their defense and security policies, represents a significant introduction to new dynamics and forces in the global geopolitical arena. The diversity and complexity of security challenges faced by BRICS countries, coupled with their global and regional ambitions, generate an intricate fabric of collaboration, competition, and, in some cases, confrontation.

Bilateral and Multilateral Strategies BRICS defense and security policies are shaped through a blend of bilateral and multilateral strategies, seeking to balance the inherent tensions between national sovereignty and international cooperation. This intricate balancing act is evident in various alliances, security agreements, and diplomatic commitments, both within the BRICS bloc and with other nations and regional blocs.

Innovations in the Defense Sector From a military and technological standpoint, BRICS nations have made significant strides, dedicating substantial resources to the development of advanced military capabilities and the adoption of emerging technologies. This not only strengthens their defensive capabilities but also projects an image of military power that can be used as a tool for geopolitical influence and deterrence.

Power Dynamics The power dynamics between the BRICS and established Western countries, particularly the United States and NATO allies, represent an ongoing dance of cooperation and rivalry. In various theaters, such as the Middle East and Asia, the BRICS seek to assert their influence, sometimes in contrast to Western interests, creating an evolving geopolitical balance.

Challenges of Globalization and Common Security Globalization and transnational challenges, such as terrorism, asymmetric conflicts, and cyber security, require a joint response and innovative security strategies. The connection between transnational threats and domestic security creates an environment where multilateral cooperation becomes crucial, despite rivalries and ideological differences.

Regional Stability At the regional level, BRICS countries play crucial roles in establishing or, in some cases, disrupting the balance of power, influencing peace and stability. Understanding how their defense policies impact regional and global tensions is vital for deciphering the future of international security.

Final Reflections In summary, as the BRICS assert themselves as key players in the global security context, their impact is as multifaceted as it is nuanced. The internal cohesion of the bloc, despite differences and bilateral disputes, symbolizes a concerted effort at repositioning within the global hierarchy. However, national individualities and geopolitical agendas continue to shape the distinct trajectories of their defense and security policies, offering a rich and at times contradictory landscape of alliances, rivalries, and cooperative strategies.

The future path of the BRICS, both as a collective entity and as individual nations, remains a journey laden with potentials, challenges, and uncertainties, requiring careful navigation through the intricate corridors of global defense and security politics. Analyzing and understanding the nuances of their policies, strategies, and alliances will be crucial to discerning the direction of the emerging new world order and the implications of these powers in the context of global stability and security.

Impact of BRICS Cultures and Societies on the World

The impact of the cultures and societies of BRICS countries on the world is immense and multidimensional, permeating various sectors, from the economic to the political, and influencing global discourses on development, human rights, and cultural diversity. The cultures of the BRICS, given their historical, demographic, and social roots, present a mosaic of traditions, practices, languages, and beliefs that profoundly influence the global landscape.

Diversity and Cultural Richness

1. **Linguistic and Religious Diversity:**

   - The BRICS host a myriad of languages and religions, creating a cultural mosaic that informs and enriches global dialogues on tolerance and diversity.

2. **Heritage and History:**

   - Each BRICS nation boasts a rich cultural and historical heritage, often reflecting ancient civilizations and deep traditions that have shaped global societies over centuries.

Art and Cultural Expression

3. **Cinema and Media:**

- Countries like India, with Bollywood, and Brazil, with its vibrant film and television expressions, have permeated global popular culture, influencing aesthetics and global narratives.

4. **Art and Literature:**

- Artists and writers from the BRICS have significantly impacted global cultural and artistic discourses, bringing diverse perspectives and storytelling to the world of arts.

Social and Demographic Influence

5. **Population Dynamics:**

- The large populations of countries like China and India not only drive global markets but also the spread and adoption of cultural and social trends.

6. **Migrations and Diaspora:**

- The vast diasporas of BRICS nations worldwide act as cultural bridges, facilitating cultural exchange and integration across different regions of the world.

Education and Research

7. **Academic Exchanges and Research:**

   - BRICS academic institutions make significant contributions to global research and academic exchanges, promoting knowledge and cultural, scientific, and technological innovations.

Politics and Society

8. **Social Models:**

   - Social and political models, such as China's economic development model, have influenced global discourses on development and governance.

9. **Civil Rights Movements:**

   - Movements like the anti-apartheid struggle in South Africa serve as inspiration and reference points for global struggles for civil rights and justice.

Cuisine and Gastronomy

10. **Global Cuisine:**

    - The cuisines of BRICS nations have influenced palates and kitchens worldwide, making dishes like Indian curry or Brazilian feijoada globally recognized.

Fashion and Style

11. Fashion and Design:

- BRICS designers and stylists have influenced the fashion and design industry, bringing unique fabrics, styles, and trends to the global stage.

Tourism and Cultural Exchanges

12. Tourism and Exploration:

- Places like China with its Great Wall and Brazil with its iconic Christ the Redeemer attract visitors from around the world, promoting cultural exchanges and mutual understanding.

In summary, the societies and cultures of BRICS, with their uniqueness and diversity, have woven pervasive and lasting influence through the socio-cultural fabric of the world, continuously shaping and enriching global dialogues and interactions in multiple ways. Their influence is not confined to a single dimension but branches through a multitude of sectors, defining and redefining global dynamics and currents in ways that are both tangible and subtle, projecting their voices and values far beyond their national borders.

The importance of BRICS in the global cultural and social context can be further dissected by exploring various key aspects that highlight the depth and breadth of their global influences.

Languages and Literatures of BRICS

The impact of the languages and literatures of BRICS cannot be underestimated. For example, Russian literature, with pioneering works by authors like Tolstoy and Dostoevsky, has offered the world profound insights into the complexities of the human psyche and society. Similarly, India's rich linguistic tapestry, comprising a vast number of languages and dialects, becomes a catalyst for preserving and promoting immeasurable cultural diversity, fueling dialogues and narratives on multiple levels and creating bridges of intercultural understanding.

Philosophies and Beliefs of BRICS

The philosophies and beliefs rooted in BRICS nations have also generated a tremendous global impact. Indian philosophy, for instance, with its numerous streams of thought, has explored the nature of existence and reality in ways that have influenced not only the East but also Western thought in terms of spirituality and metaphysics. Similarly, Chinese Confucianism has provided an ethical and moral framework that has influenced governance and social relations throughout East Asia and beyond.

Festivals and Traditions of BRICS

The festivals and traditions of BRICS nations offer another layer of cultural influence. For example, the Brazilian Carnival and the Chinese Lantern Festival are not only cultural celebrations within their respective countries but have become global events attracting international visitors and influencing cultural celebrations and artistic expressions worldwide. They symbolize the expression of joy, unity, and the continuation of traditions across generations, serving as vital links between the past, present, and future.

BRICS in the Global Creative Economy

The presence of BRICS in the global creative economy is another domain deserving attention. India, with its robust software industry, and China, with its massive manufacturing sector, have influenced not only global markets but also worldwide business practices and strategies. This, in turn, has shaped the dynamics of the global economies and defined new paths for international collaboration and competition.

Role of Women in BRICS Societies

The role of women in BRICS societies and their global impact is another significant dimension. Figures like Indira Gandhi in India and Dilma Rousseff in Brazil have taken on leadership roles and influenced policies and discourses both nationally and internationally. Their experiences, challenges, and triumphs serve as models and inspiration for women and girls worldwide, elevating discussions on women's rights and gender equality on the global stage.

Music and Dance of BRICS

Furthermore, the influence of BRICS music and dance extends far beyond their national borders. Brazilian samba, Indian Kathak, and Russian ballet are just a few examples of how BRICS' artistic forms have crossed geographical boundaries, becoming integral parts of global culture and offering the world a wealth of artistic and creative expressions.

The multifaceted nature of BRICS societies and cultures not only enriches their internal socio-cultural fabric but also extends their influential hands across the globe, intertwining with and influencing the global cultural and social map in various profound ways. In every sphere, from the arts to philosophies, traditions to innovations, BRICS continue to play a crucial role in shaping and directing global cultural and social currents, building bridges of understanding, collaboration, and exchange in an increasingly interconnected and interdependent world.

Cuisine and Gastronomy of BRICS

Another area in which BRICS manifest a remarkable global influence is cuisine. The vastness and diversity of culinary traditions in these nations are reflected in a wealth of flavors, techniques, and ingredients that have been widely adopted and adapted worldwide. Consider, for example, Indian cuisine, celebrated for its skillful use of spices and aromatic herbs, which has led to the creation of internationally renowned dishes such as curry or biryani. Observing Brazilian cuisine, feijoada, a dish made from black beans and meat, exemplifies the fusion of culinary influences that characterizes the nation, skillfully exploring and blending indigenous, African, and Portuguese cultural roots.

Cinematography of BRICS

Cinema is another medium through which BRICS convey their culture and society, exerting significant influence on a global scale. India's Bollywood film industry, for instance, not only has a substantial cultural impact domestically but also enjoys a wide international following, with a fan base that extends from London to Lagos. Similarly, Chinese cinema has gained international resonance, showcasing not only China's rich history and culture but also its modernization and current social and political dynamics to the world.

Cultural Tourism

Cultural tourism is another sector in which BRICS have had a significant impact, with each nation attracting visitors from around the world eager to explore their rich historical and cultural offerings. Cities like Rio de Janeiro in Brazil and St. Petersburg in Russia are celebrated for their invaluable cultural heritage, offering tourists insights into the historical roots and vibrant modernity of these nations. These places become crucibles of cultural exchange and points of connection between BRICS citizens and the rest of the world, fostering mutual understanding and respect among diverse cultures and peoples.

Technological and Societal Innovations

BRICS are also significant drivers of technological and societal innovations that influence societies globally. Innovations in ICT from India, for example, have not only propelled the nation toward a digital future but have also offered technological solutions to developing countries worldwide. China's innovations in infrastructure and technology, such as the Alipay digital payment system, have influenced how societies handle financial transactions and economic interactions, suggesting new models and practices that could be adopted and adapted in various global contexts.

Education and Research

Education and research in BRICS nations also play a crucial role in shaping the global future. Educational institutions in these countries not only educate the future generations of leaders, thinkers, and innovators but also develop research and innovations that have the potential to address global challenges in fields such as medicine, technology, and environmental sciences.

Social Movements

Finally, social movements within BRICS nations often have a resonating global echo, providing insights and inspiration for international discussions and actions. Whether related to gender issues, the environment, or human rights, such movements reflect the dynamics, challenges, and aspirations of BRICS societies, serving as mirrors through which these nations present themselves and are perceived globally.

Through these numerous facets, the cultures and societies of BRICS intertwine and interact with the global landscape, contributing to shaping not only their own future but also that of the entire global community.

Summary, Cultural and Societal Aspects of BRICS Nations

In summary, the culture and society of BRICS nations weave a complex and diverse tapestry of influences and interactions that permeate the global stage in multiple ways.

Global Cultural Heritage

Each BRICS member country contributes uniquely to the global cultural heritage through art, music, literature, and traditions that are historically rooted yet continually evolving. This cultural heritage not only enriches the fabric of each country's history and identity but also intertwines with global cultures, creating new points of interconnectedness and intercultural dialogue.

Cultural Synergies and Frictions

The plurality of cultural and social expressions among BRICS nations generates both synergies and frictions. Synergies emerge through the sharing and mutual adaptation of cultural ideas and practices, while frictions can arise from ideological divergences, disparities in soft power, and varying priorities in cultural and social policies.

Amplifiers of Social Change

BRICS societies also act as amplifiers of social change, offering new narratives and paradigms that challenge the status quo both nationally and internationally. This occurs through social movements, cultural and political activism initiatives, and the creation and dissemination of media and artistic content that convey powerful and often transformative messages.

Integration and Divergence

BRICS, with their distinct cultures and societies, stand at a crossroads of integration and divergence. On one hand, multilateral cooperation in various sectors promotes integration and the sharing of common goals. On the other hand, divergences become evident in different trajectories of social and cultural development, diverse approaches to governance and conflict resolution, and varying perceptions and responses to global challenges.

Cultural Leadership

BRICS nations are striving to assert cultural leadership, projecting their values, narratives, and cultural practices beyond their borders. This leadership manifests through various channels, such as film productions, international cultural events, and the promotion of native languages on the global stage.

Towards the Future

Finally, the projection of BRICS towards the future is embedded in their collective and individual efforts to forge sustainable and inclusive paths of social and cultural development. This involves promoting innovations, adopting emerging technologies, and committing to greater equity and inclusion within their own societies and on the international stage.

In the ultimate analysis, as BRICS continue to explore new frontiers of cooperation and navigate the intrinsic challenges of their diverse cultural and social identities, mutual understanding and respect for shared values will be crucial in forging a common and constructive future both within the bloc and in the broader global context. The analysis of culture and society within BRICS provides a window through which to explore the dynamics and potential of this influential group of nations on the world stage.

14. Financial Institutions, Role of BRICS Financial Institutions such as the BRICS Bank

The role of financial institutions in BRICS nations, such as the BRICS Bank, is fundamental in shaping the economic and financial landscape not only within the bloc but also globally.

BRICS Bank: A Pillar of Economic Development

The BRICS Bank, officially known as the New Development Bank (NDB), was established in 2014 as a direct response to the need for a new financial mechanism that could support infrastructure and sustainable development projects in emerging economies and developing countries. The NDB plays a key role in:

- **Financing Infrastructure Projects:** It provides funding and support for infrastructure and sustainable development projects within BRICS countries.

- **Financial Cooperation:** It serves as a platform for financial cooperation among its members, facilitating trade and investment through the creation of shared and collaborative financial mechanisms.

- **Complement and Alternative:** It acts as a complement and alternative to existing financial institutions, specifically addressing the needs and dynamics of BRICS countries and other emerging economies.

Multidimensional Role of BRICS Financial Institutions

1. **Economic Growth Catalyst:** BRICS financial institutions play a strategic role in catalyzing economic growth by financing projects and initiatives that can improve infrastructure and create investment opportunities.

2. **Poverty Reduction and Sustainable Development:** They are essential in driving efforts toward poverty reduction and sustainable development, providing resources and technical support for projects and policies that promote social and economic inclusion.

3. **Economic Stabilization:** They serve as economic stabilizers, helping to mitigate economic vulnerabilities through fund provision and the implementation of coordinated financial policies during times of crisis.

4. **Trade and Investments:** They act as facilitators of trade and investments, creating platforms and mechanisms that make it easier and more convenient for member states to collaborate and invest mutually.

Future Prospects and Challenges

- **Equity and Transparency:** Ensuring that resources and benefits from financial institutions are distributed fairly and transparently among all members.

- **Governance and Accountability:** Implementing strong and transparent governance mechanisms that ensure accountability and effectiveness of financial institutions.

- **Adaptability and Resilience:** Evolving and adapting to changing global economic dynamics, ensuring that financial institutions remain resilient in the face of future challenges.

- **Global Collaboration:** Promoting closer collaboration with other international and regional financial institutions.

In Summary

Financial institutions within the BRICS, such as the BRICS Bank, represent a fundamental pillar for supporting and promoting sustainable and integrated economic development among member countries and beyond. Their ability to navigate challenges and capitalize on opportunities will largely determine the future of economic and financial cooperation within the BRICS bloc and in the broader global financial system.

Continuing the discussion on the importance of financial institutions within the BRICS bloc, it becomes evident how the interplay of economic, social, and political elements is central in analyzing these institutions' capacity to influence global geopolitics and economics.

Financial Integration

Financial integration among BRICS countries is crucial for the overall strength and resilience of the bloc. This integration extends beyond infrastructure project financing to the creation of a robust and interconnected financial system that can cater to the specific needs of member countries. Furthermore, the establishment of a BRICS payment system that facilitates trade transactions within the bloc represents another critical aspect of enhancing financial and economic integration among member countries.

Private Sector Development

BRICS financial institutions also play an essential role in private sector development within member countries by providing funding and support to small and medium-sized enterprises (SMEs) and initiating projects that can drive innovation and entrepreneurship. In this context, SMEs and emerging startups can access capital and resources that would otherwise be challenging to obtain, thus stimulating innovation, job creation, and economic growth.

Interaction with Global Economies

It is also relevant to consider the interaction of BRICS financial institutions with global economies and how they influence and are influenced by international economic and financial dynamics. The ability of BRICS financial institutions to navigate the ups and downs of the global economy while ensuring the stability and growth of member countries is a key element in building a more balanced and sustainable global financial system.

Challenges in Project Implementation

Challenges in local and regional project implementation are also a key area to examine. Despite the availability of funds and resources, there are often bureaucratic, technical, and social obstacles that hinder the effective implementation of infrastructure and development projects. In this regard, BRICS financial institutions must not only ensure the availability of capital but also facilitate project realization by offering technical expertise, managing socio-environmental issues, and overcoming bureaucratic hurdles.

Environmental and Social Implications

The environmental and social implications of projects funded by BRICS financial institutions are another crucial point to consider. Financing large-scale infrastructure projects can have significant impacts on the environment and local communities. Therefore, it is imperative for financial institutions to adopt a responsible and sustainable approach to investment, ensuring that projects are both economically beneficial and environmentally and socially sustainable.

Internal Power Dynamics

Analyzing internal power dynamics within BRICS financial institutions and how they influence decision-making and policies is also a critical element. The distribution of decision-making power, tensions, and alliances among member countries, and how these dynamics are reflected in the operations and initiatives of financial institutions, offer valuable insights into the functionality and effectiveness of such institutions in the long term.

In conclusion, while these are just some of the many facets that characterize the role of BRICS financial institutions, it is clear that their influence goes well beyond simple project financing. They are agents of development, facilitators of international cooperation, and influential players in the global economic stage, with all the complexities and challenges that entails.

Further underscoring the importance of financial institutions within the BRICS bloc, various critical aspects and dynamics influencing and influenced by these entities can be explored.

Cooperation and International Competition

Examining the international landscape, BRICS financial institutions play a dual role of cooperation and competition. On one hand, they seek to develop synergies with existing global financial institutions, such as the International Monetary Fund and the World Bank, attempting to navigate and at times challenge prevailing power dynamics. On the other hand, they represent a form of antagonism toward the dominant global financial system, offering an alternative or counterbalance to Western financial institutions and their funding and development models.

Diversification of Investment Portfolios

Another sphere of interest could be the management and diversification of investment portfolios by BRICS financial institutions. How are projects selected to receive funding? What are the policies and practices adopted to mitigate risks and ensure a return on investment? Risk management, project feasibility analysis, and the creation of a sustainable investment strategy are essential to ensure that funding is distributed effectively and has a positive impact on the economic development of member countries and beyond.

Focusing on Specific Sectors

An examination of specific sectors favored by BRICS financial institutions could provide insights into where the bloc sees the greatest opportunities and challenges. For example, attention can be placed on renewable energy, infrastructure construction, sustainable agriculture, or digitalization, each of which comes with specific sets of benefits, challenges, and implementation dynamics.

Social Impacts of Financed Projects

Analyzing the social impacts of projects financed by BRICS financial institutions is an area that deserves careful scrutiny. This includes assessing the projects' impact on the socio-economic well-being of local communities, job creation, poverty reduction, and gender equality. Additionally, exploring how these institutions address issues of inclusion and social justice in their investment projects and financial policies would be interesting.

Regulations and Compliance

Regulatory compliance and legal challenges represent another fundamental aspect of the operations of BRICS financial institutions. This entails not only complying with local laws and regulations in the countries where they operate but also adhering to international standards related to transparency, anti-corruption, and environmental norms. Exploring the strategies and measures adopted to ensure that financed projects comply with relevant laws and regulations is vital for understanding the challenges and opportunities that BRICS financial institutions encounter in global project financing.

Financial Inclusion

Financial inclusion is another dimension that could be further explored. How do BRICS financial institutions contribute to promoting financial inclusion in member countries and beneficiary nations of their financing? The adoption of financial technologies (FinTech) and initiatives to extend financial services to unbanked or underbanked communities are some of the mechanisms through which these institutions can promote greater financial inclusion and equality.

Partial Conclusions and Future Perspectives

While each aspect could be further expanded, it is essential to recognize that BRICS financial institutions operate in a complex and ever-evolving global environment. As they work to finance projects that fuel growth and development in member countries and partner nations, these institutions must balance development goals, sustainability, and investment returns, all while navigating the complexities of global geopolitics and economic dynamics.

The ability of BRICS financial institutions to adapt, innovate, and develop effective mechanisms for risk management and capitalizing on opportunities will be fundamental to their success and impact on the future of global development financing. Over time, the role, influence, and impact of these institutions will be shaped by the strategic decisions made today and their ability to respond in an agile and innovative manner to emerging challenges.

Financial Integration and Stability

BRICS financial institutions play an essential role in integrating financial markets and ensuring stability within the bloc. By creating a platform that aims to facilitate trade and direct investments among member countries, these institutions seek to stabilize and enhance national economies in a global context. Financial integration and stability help member countries protect themselves against external vulnerabilities, offering greater resilience against global market fluctuations and economic crises.

Partnerships and Private Sector Engagement

Engaging the private sector through partnerships with BRICS financial institutions is critical for mobilizing additional capital and technical expertise. BRICS financial institutions, such as the BRICS Bank, often seek to attract private investors and establish partnerships with the private sector to amplify the impact of their projects and programs. A detailed analysis of how these institutions collaborate with the private sector and engage investors and companies can provide insights into the effectiveness and sustainability of funded projects.

Small and Medium-sized Enterprises (SMEs) Development

SMEs play a crucial role in BRICS economies, significantly contributing to economic growth, job creation, and sustainable development. Therefore, BRICS financial institutions could develop strategies to support SMEs by providing funding, training, and technical assistance. How are these programs structured? How do they contribute to improving the entrepreneurial ecosystem in member countries?

Transparency and Accountability

The issue of transparency and accountability in BRICS financial institutions is another aspect worthy of in-depth examination. This includes not only internal operations but also decision-making processes, fund allocation, and project management. Examining the measures and practices adopted by BRICS financial institutions to ensure transparency and accountability toward member countries and project beneficiaries is crucial for assessing their impact and effectiveness.

Sustainable Development and Green Finance

Furthermore, an analysis of the commitment of BRICS financial institutions to sustainable development and green finance is of vital importance. What green financial instruments are these institutions exploring or have implemented? How are projects evaluated and monitored from an environmental sustainability perspective? A deep dive into strategies and approaches to green finance and sustainable development could provide insights into how the BRICS are addressing issues related to climate change and sustainability through their financial institutions.

Governance and Organizational Structure

Governance and the organizational structure of BRICS financial institutions also warrant a thorough examination. How are policies formulated? Who makes decisions and through what mechanisms? How does the governance structure influence the setting of priorities and project implementation? Analyzing the structure and decision-making mechanisms can help gain a better understanding of how these institutions operate and how they may evolve in the future.

Open Conclusion

Continuing to explore and delve into these and other aspects of BRICS financial institutions leads to a journey of discovery intertwined with increasingly broad and intricate themes, where finance, development, politics, and sustainability converge into a global network of interconnections and interdependencies, with implications that extend far beyond the borders of member countries and are rooted in an ever-changing and renegotiating international system.

Contextualizing BRICS Financial Institutions

BRICS financial institutions, particularly the BRICS Bank, have assumed a pivotal role in supporting and driving economic development, not only in member countries but also in other emerging markets. The creation of a solid and resilient financial platform allows BRICS countries to pursue broader development goals, collectively address economic challenges, and forge an influential role in the global economic system.

Economic Development and Project Financing

Financial institutions, through the development and financing of various projects in key sectors such as infrastructure, energy, and sustainable development, become pillars of economic progress and stability. These projects, in addition to providing direct stimuli to local economies, facilitate intra-BRICS trade and investments, strengthening economic networks and partnerships among member countries.

Engagement with Local Communities

The involvement and impact of BRICS financial institutions on local communities are essential aspects. Financed and developed projects should not only respect the rights and needs of local communities but also contribute to their well-being and development. How these institutions engage with local communities, adopt sustainable practices, and assess the social and environmental impact of projects is crucial for understanding their responsibility and effectiveness in promoting genuine and inclusive development.

Innovation and Financial Technology

Innovation and the adoption of new financial technologies represent another key point. BRICS financial institutions are exploring and adopting emerging technologies such as blockchain and cryptocurrencies to enhance efficiency, reduce costs, and increase transparency in financial transactions and operations. The position of BRICS in the fintech field and the future implications of such innovations in global finance and development practices deserve detailed analysis.

Dialogue and International Cooperation

Furthermore, BRICS financial institutions operate not only within the bloc but also in a broader international context. Their ability to engage in dialogue and cooperate with other international financial institutions, such as the International Monetary Fund and the World Bank, and the position they take in global economic forums, contribute to defining the role and influence of BRICS in the global economic landscape.

Conclusions and Future Perspectives

BRICS financial institutions, challenging traditional financial mechanisms and positioning themselves as alternatives and/or complements to Western financial institutions, are gradually shaping a new economic and financial landscape. Balancing the pursuit of domestic development goals, maintaining economic stability and growth, and navigating the complex waters of geopolitics and international alliances define a complex and multifaceted path.

Exploring the future trajectory of BRICS, the dynamics within the bloc, their ability to balance national and collective interests, and to promote sustainable and inclusive development, will significantly determine the future global economic and financial order.

Therefore, a landscape of opportunities and challenges emerges, in which BRICS, through their financial institutions, will continue to navigate, shaping and being shaped by the global context in which they operate. Their trajectory, if able to balance national and collective interests and promote development that is sustainable and inclusive, will significantly shape the future global economic and financial order.

International Trade • Analyzing the Role of BRICS in International Trade

The Evolution of International Trade through BRICS

The BRICS bloc (Brazil, Russia, India, China, and South Africa) has assumed an increasingly influential role in the international trade landscape, contributing to redefining global dynamics and forming new trade corridors and economic alliances. Their position in the world economy, intra-bloc trade, and foreign trade strategies are all critical elements for understanding how BRICS is shaping and being shaped by international trade dynamics.

Economic Impact and Global Relevance

BRICS nations, despite their economic size, natural resources, and socio-economic structures, share the common goal of increasing their influence in the global trade arena. The growing significance of these countries in global exports, their increasing weight in the world economy, and their role in the production and distribution of goods globally mark a decisive influence in global value chains.

Trade Dynamics Within BRICS

Within the BRICS framework, member countries have sought to intensify mutual trade, aiming to reduce dependence on advanced economies and diversify their own economies. This strategy has led to increased economic integration among bloc countries, through bilateral and multilateral agreements, trade facilitation, and the establishment of common platforms for economic dialogue and cooperation.

Global Integration Strategies

BRICS, in their quest to consolidate their position in global trade, have also explored strategies of integration and cooperation with other emerging and developed economies. The formation of regional alliances, such as China's Belt and Road Initiative (BRI), and participation in multilateral economic forums, are expressions of these nations' willingness to build extensive and resilient trade networks.

Challenges and Opportunities

However, BRICS face various challenges in pursuing sustainable trade growth and balancing their economic ambitions with internal development needs and environmental sustainability. Trade tensions, policy divergences, and structural differences among member countries' economies represent significant obstacles that require shared solutions and continuous dialogue.

Sustainability Dimension in Trade

Sustainability in trade, namely the ability of BRICS to promote trade that is not only economically advantageous but also socially and environmentally responsible, emerges as a central theme. The environmental impact of trade, labor practices, and technology transfer are all factors that influence and are influenced by the trade dynamics of BRICS and require in-depth analysis to understand and guide the future trajectories of the bloc.

Towards the Future of Global Trade

In summary, with their growing economic and trade influence, BRICS are shaping a new order in international trade, proposing new dynamics, creating new alliances, and, in a way, redesigning the maps of global trade routes. Their ability to navigate internal and external challenges, promote sustainable and inclusive trade, and balance their economic ambitions with global needs will determine the future of their role in international trade and the imprint of their impact on the global economy.

In this context, future analysis of BRICS in international trade, through the exploration of their trade policies, global integration strategies, and the management of emerging challenges and opportunities, will provide crucial insights into understanding the future evolutions of global trade and the international economic system.

Influence of BRICS in International Organizations

BRICS nations are not only active in defining new trade paths but also play an increasingly prominent role in international trade institutions and organizations, such as the World Trade Organization (WTO). Their often unified position in these forums allows them to influence international trade norms and agreements, seeking to better reflect the interests and needs of emerging economies.

Technology and Digital Trade

Furthermore, the increasing digitization of global trade represents both an opportunity and a challenge for BRICS countries. On one hand, e-commerce and digital platforms offer new channels and markets for goods and services, helping to overcome physical and logistical barriers. On the other hand, digitization requires adapting technological infrastructure, cybersecurity regulations, and digital skills.

Investment Policies

The foreign direct investment (FDI) strategies of BRICS, both in terms of inbound and outbound investments, are another pillar of their trade activity. Creating policies that attract foreign investments and, at the same time, identifying opportunities for foreign investment are essential for maintaining and increasing economic growth and establishing strong and mutual trade relationships.

Relations with Developing Countries

The role of BRICS in the global South is also significant. Many developing countries view BRICS as preferred partners because they can offer alternative growth models to those proposed by advanced economies, sometimes with fewer political conditions. This has allowed BRICS to build networks of influence and partnerships in Asia, Africa, and Latin America, further strengthening their weight in global trade.

Contradictions and Criticisms

Despite the significant impact of BRICS, numerous contradictions and criticisms exist. Inequalities within BRICS countries are often accentuated, and export-oriented growth strategies can sometimes conflict with the need to develop robust and inclusive domestic markets. The challenge lies in balancing export-oriented policies with strategies that ensure equitable distribution of the benefits of growth at the national level.

Environmental Issues and Sustainability

Environmental issues are another fundamental aspect to consider. The intensification of trade can have a significant impact on the environment, both in terms of emissions generated by transportation and the exploitation of natural resources. Therefore, BRICS are called upon to reflect on how to reconcile the need for growth and development with the need to protect the environment and promote sustainable development.

The Pandemic and New Dynamics

Finally, the impact of the COVID-19 pandemic has rewritten many of the rules of international trade, prompting a reflection on the vulnerabilities and resilience of global supply chains. For BRICS, which have managed the crisis with different approaches and have been affected in different ways, the post-pandemic period will be a key time to reconsider and potentially reformulate their trade and development strategies.

All these aspects outline a complex and multidimensional landscape in which BRICS navigate while seeking to consolidate their role, facing rapidly evolving global dynamics and internal challenges that require attention and strategic balance.

Continuing to Explore the Broader Landscape of BRICS in the Context of International Trade

It is essential to consider several other aspects that highlight the nuances and complexity of their interactions in the global system while continuing to explore the extensive scenario of BRICS in the context of international trade.

Bilateralism and Multilateralism

While acting as a bloc in some circumstances, BRICS also aggressively pursue national interests through bilateral agreements, both within the group and with other countries and regions. The tension between bilateralism and multilateralism is ever-present: while multilateralism may offer more equitable and sustainable global solutions, bilateral agreements often allow countries to more directly pursue their national interests.

Tariff and Non-Tariff Policies

BRICS employ a variety of tariff and non-tariff tools to protect their industries and domestic markets and to promote or inhibit specific trade flows. The use of such instruments can reflect both economic and political objectives and, in some cases, can also be used as a tool of geopolitical pressure.

Labor Rights Norms

Another essential element concerns labor rights in BRICS countries. Due to the diversity of economic and social situations in each country, regulations and working conditions vary significantly, influencing competition and production and trade dynamics within and outside the group.

Soft Power and Image Building

BRICS also use trade as a means to build their "soft power" and influence other countries through economic cooperation and the development of common markets. By creating economic networks and joint initiatives, they seek to strengthen their influence and shape global perceptions of them.

Financial Market Integration

Integration of financial markets and currency policies among BRICS countries is also of fundamental importance. The use of their own currencies for trade within the group and the interconnection of their stock exchanges and financial institutions represent both opportunities for stability and potential vectors of contagion in case of financial crises.

Infrastructure and Logistics

Infrastructure and logistics play a vital role in facilitating or hindering international trade. Infrastructure projects, such as China's Belt and Road Initiative, not only create new trade routes but also serve as instruments of geopolitical influence, economically and physically connecting various regions of the world.

Trade and Human Rights

The relationship between trade and human rights is another thorny issue often brought to the forefront in terms of BRICS' external relations. Balancing commercial and economic interests with respect for human rights and the promotion of global standards is a persistent dilemma and a source of tension both internally and in international relations.

Patents and Intellectual Property

Finally, issues related to patents and intellectual property, especially in the era of technology and biotechnology, represent fertile ground for potential conflicts and collaborations. How BRICS manage their intellectual property policies not only influences dynamics within the group but also has broader implications for innovation, access to technologies and medicines, and relations with other countries and multinational corporations.

These additional aspects offer an even more detailed and complex framework of the dynamics that drive BRICS in the context of international trade, outlining a landscape of intertwined relationships, sometimes conflicting objectives, and a continuous navigation between cooperation and competition.

In Conclusion

In conclusion, the analysis of the role of BRICS in international trade reveals an extraordinarily complex and dynamic reality. These countries, despite their differences and internal challenges, have demonstrated a significant impact on the global stage, redefining trade dynamics and contributing to shaping a new world order.

BRICS have grown in importance in the global economy, becoming among the leading players in international trade. Their influence has been evident in various sectors, from energy and commodities to high technology and manufacturing. Foreign trade strategies, economic diversification, and the creation of global trade networks have become distinctive features of their approach to international trade.

However, BRICS face numerous challenges, such as internal inequalities, environmental issues, divergences in economic policies, and difficulties in managing complex relationships with other global actors. Striking a balance between promoting fair and sustainable trade and achieving national economic goals remains a constant dilemma.

The post-pandemic period will be crucial for BRICS to redefine their trade and development strategies in light of new global dynamics. It will be essential to consider how to address emerging challenges, including climate change, the digitization of trade, and the need to promote inclusive and sustainable growth.

Ultimately, BRICS will remain a key player in international trade and continue to shape the new world order. Their ability to adapt to evolving challenges and contribute to shared and sustainable economic growth will determine their future success and lasting impact on the global stage.

16. Globalization vs. Nationalism • Discussion on How BRICS Balance Globalization and Nationalism

The discussion on how BRICS balance globalization and nationalism is of paramount importance as it reflects one of the most relevant challenges in today's geopolitical landscape. These emerging countries navigate between the desire to actively participate in economic globalization and the need to preserve national sovereignty and cultural identity. Here are some key points to understand this complex dynamic:

Economic Globalization

BRICS have generally adopted a favorable position towards economic globalization. They recognize the benefits of participating in global markets, such as access to new markets, foreign investment flows, and the importation of advanced technologies. They have promoted trade agreements, investment exchanges, and economic partnerships with other nations, demonstrating a willingness to deepen international trade ties.

Moderate Protectionism

However, BRICS are not strangers to moderate protectionism, especially concerning strategic sectors or the defense of national interests. They use tools such as tariffs, import quotas, and regulations to protect local industries and promote domestic production. These measures can be employed in response to economic crises or geopolitical pressures.

Cultural Nationalism

From a cultural and political perspective, BRICS are committed to preserving and promoting their national and cultural identities. Each of these countries has a unique history, language, and culture and seeks to shield them from the cultural homogenization brought by globalization. This cultural nationalism can manifest in policies promoting language, arts, and national culture.

Political Sovereignty

BRICS maintain a strong stance on political sovereignty. They reject external interference in internal affairs and uphold the principle of non-interference in the affairs of other countries. This position is often expressed concerning issues such as regional tensions, internal conflicts, and regime changes.

Emphasized Balance

BRICS constantly seek a balance between active participation in economic globalization and the defense of their national and cultural interests. This balance is often challenged by global events, such as financial crises, geopolitical conflicts, and trade tensions. In such moments, they may adopt a more nationalist or more globalized position depending on the circumstances.

In summary, BRICS represent a challenge to the traditional dichotomy between globalization and nationalism. These countries strive to balance active participation in economic globalization with the protection of their national and cultural interests. Their ability to maintain this delicate equilibrium will be fundamental to their future and the definition of the role of emerging economies in the global context.

To gain a more detailed understanding of how BRICS balance globalization and nationalism, it's important to examine specific examples and the challenges associated with this complex dynamic:

1. International Trade

BRICS have favored the liberalization of international trade but also protect key sectors of their economies from excessive competition. For example, Brazil has imposed tariffs on certain manufactured products to protect its domestic industry, while India has adopted similar policies to support the agricultural sector. These actions have often been a subject of controversy as they can hinder full adherence to global trade.

2. Foreign Investments

BRICS have attracted substantial foreign investments but have become more selective in allowing access to strategic sectors. For instance, China has tightened oversight of foreign direct investments in areas like technology and national security. This move is seen as an attempt to balance the need for foreign capital with the preservation of national security and key technologies.

3. Technology and Data Control

BRICS are actively engaged in the global technology race but also seek to ensure their technological independence and data security. For example, Russia has enacted a law requiring personal data of Russian citizens to be stored on servers located within the country, a move interpreted as an effort to increase control over data and technology.

4. Cultural Identity

BRICS place significant importance on promoting their unique cultural identities. This translates into policies supporting language, arts, and national culture. For example, Brazil promotes the spread of the Portuguese language, while India supports the spread of the Hindi language. These efforts reflect a commitment to preserving cultural diversity in an increasingly globalized world.

5. Global Leadership

BRICS actively seek to expand their influence on the global stage. They collaborate in organizations like the United Nations and the G20 to promote a more multipolar world order. However, they are also committed to supporting the principle of national sovereignty and avoiding interference in the internal affairs of other countries.

6. Geopolitical Challenges

Geopolitical challenges such as the conflict in Ukraine and tensions between India and China in the Himalayas have tested the solidarity of BRICS. While they seek to balance their bilateral relationships with other global actors like the United States and the

European Union, they must address geopolitical challenges that test their approach to sovereignty and global cooperation.

In summary, BRICS constantly face a complex set of challenges when it comes to balancing globalization with nationalism. Their policies and actions depend on a range of factors, including economic interests, geopolitical challenges, and the desire to preserve their cultural identities. This dynamic is at the heart of their global relations and represents one of the most significant challenges in the current geopolitical context.

7. **Natural Resources** The BRICS countries are rich in natural resources, and this is a factor that influences their economic and trade policies. While they seek to benefit from globalization by exporting resources, they also adopt policies to protect and strategically manage these resources. For example, Brazil has policies for controlling the exports of natural resources like oil, while Russia has similar limitations on natural gas exports.

8. **Infrastructure Investments** The BRICS have initiated significant infrastructure investment projects, both at the national and international levels. These investments are often aimed at promoting regional and global connectivity and supporting economic growth. However, such

projects can also be used as tools of geopolitical influence, contributing to the creation of trade networks and the consolidation of the BRICS' global influence.

9. **Pandemic and Health Nationalism** The COVID-19 pandemic has reignited the debate on globalization and nationalism. While the BRICS have collaborated to ensure access to vaccines and share scientific knowledge, each country has also adopted national measures to protect the health of its citizens. This balance between global cooperation and health protectionism exemplifies the broader dilemma between globalization and nationalism.

10. **Financial Crisis Containment** The BRICS have created their own currency reserve fund, known as the "Contingent Reserve Arrangement," to address global financial crises without relying on Western financial institutions like the International Monetary Fund (IMF). This demonstrates a willingness to maintain a degree of control over their financial affairs and a preference for regional solutions over global institutions.

11. **Trade Tensions** Trade tensions among the BRICS can test the group's solidarity. For example, India and China have had trade and territorial disputes that have influenced their relations within the BRICS. These conflicts require a delicate balance

between supporting their own sovereignty and the importance of group cohesion.

12. **Geographic and Economic Diversity** The BRICS represent significant geographic and economic diversity, which further complicates the balance between globalization and nationalism. For instance, India is one of the world's largest emerging economies, while South Africa is relatively smaller. These differences influence the strategies and priorities of each country within the group.

In summary, the BRICS continue to balance globalization and nationalism through a series of policies, actions, and initiatives. This complex dynamic is shaped by economic, political, cultural, and environmental factors and requires constant adaptation to emerging challenges and opportunities in the global context. How they address this balance will have significant implications for the future of international relations and the world order.

13. **Investments in Developing Countries** The BRICS have increased investments in developing countries, both for economic and geopolitical reasons. These investments can promote economic growth in host countries but may also raise concerns about neocolonialism and economic dependency. The BRICS seek to balance their growing global

presence with the need to respect the sovereignty of host states.

14. **Economic Diplomacy** The BRICS have developed active economic diplomacy to pursue their global interests. They have organized economic and trade summits and sought to influence global organizations like the World Trade Organization (WTO) to promote their priorities. These efforts demonstrate a commitment to advancing their interests but can also create friction with other nations.

15. **Education and Science** The BRICS also collaborate in the fields of education and science to promote innovation and technological development. This cooperation can be seen as an attempt to balance globalization by promoting national education and research.

16. **Media Control** Each BRICS country has media control policies that reflect their national and cultural needs. For example, China has strict online content censorship to preserve political stability, while Brazil has regulations to promote the production of local cultural content. These approaches illustrate how the BRICS seek to balance media globalization with their national priorities.

17. **Digital Infrastructure** The BRICS have made significant progress in digital infrastructure to

reduce the digital divide. These efforts can balance globalization through universal internet access and the promotion of technological innovation at the national level.

18.   **Global Institutional Reform** The BRICS have supported the reform of global institutions, such as the United Nations Security Council, to make them more representative and responsive to contemporary challenges. This effort is an example of how they seek to influence the global system while protecting their sovereignty.

19.**Investments in Sustainable Energy** While addressing the growing energy demand, the BRICS have also made significant investments in sustainable energy, such as renewable energy sources. These investments can balance globalization by promoting cleaner energy sources and strengthening national energy security.

20.   **Coordination in International Organizations** The BRICS coordinate their positions in various international organizations, such as the G20 and the BRICS Business Council. This collaboration seeks to balance globalization through collective influence in these organizations, allowing the BRICS to promote their joint interests.

In conclusion, the balancing act between globalization and nationalism by the BRICS is a complex process involving a series of policies and initiatives. These emerging countries constantly strive to protect their national and cultural interests while actively engaging on the global stage. Their ability to manage this challenge will determine their future role in the global geopolitical and economic landscape.

21. **Food Security Measures** The BRICS have implemented policies to ensure the food security of their citizens. These policies may include promoting domestic agriculture and limiting food imports. Such measures are often justified based on the need to ensure food sovereignty but can also lead to increased protectionism.

22. **Bilateral Cultural Initiatives** Within the BRICS, countries often undertake bilateral initiatives to promote their culture. For example, Russia and India may organize cultural exchanges to enhance mutual understanding among their populations. These initiatives can help strengthen ties among member countries and preserve their cultural identities.

23. **Investments in Strategic Industries** The BRICS have identified key strategic industries for their development and seek to protect them from external influences. For example, China has adopted "Made in China 2025" policies to promote domestic high-tech industries and reduce dependence on

foreign imports. This is an example of how they balance globalization with the goal of building a technology-based economy.

24. **Shanghai Cooperation Agreement** The Shanghai Cooperation Agreement (SCO), which includes several Central Asian nations and China, is an example of how the BRICS balance regional and global interests. The SCO promotes economic and security cooperation in Central Asia, but the BRICS also use this platform to discuss global issues and coordinate their positions.

25. **Industrial and Commercial Policies** Each BRICS country has unique industrial and commercial policies to promote economic growth and employment. These policies can range from export promotion to support for small businesses. While they seek active participation in global trade, such policies also reflect efforts to maintain a degree of economic autonomy.

26. **Scientific and Technological Cooperation** The BRICS promote scientific and technological cooperation to stimulate innovation. These efforts include sharing research and jointly developing advanced technologies. Scientific collaboration reflects the BRICS' willingness to engage in global technological competition while maintaining their scientific and technological identity.

27. **Social and Environmental Impact** The
BRICS seek to balance the social and environmental
aspects of globalization. This involves addressing
challenges related to inequality and social equity, as
well as environmental issues like sustainable
resource management and climate change. These
factors contribute to the balance between
globalization and national needs.

28. **Role in Regional Forums** The BRICS actively
participate in regional forums such as the Asia-
Pacific Economic Cooperation (APEC) and the
Shanghai Cooperation Organization (SCO). This
participation reflects a multilateral approach that
balances regional and global interests.

29. **Global Economic Dependency** The BRICS
seek to balance their growing global economic
dependency with the need to preserve their
economic autonomy. This may involve diversifying
energy sources or promoting local production to
reduce dependence on imports.

30. **Soft Power Diplomacy** The BRICS aim to
promote their soft power, including cultural aspects
like literature, cinema, and art, to positively
influence global perceptions of themselves. These
efforts contribute to the promotion of their culture
and the projection of a positive image worldwide.

In conclusion, the balancing act between globalization and nationalism by the BRICS is a dynamic and complex process that requires constant attention to changes in the global context. These emerging countries are aware of the importance of actively engaging on the global stage to promote their economic, political, and cultural interests. However, at the same time, they seek to preserve their sovereignty, cultural identity, and economic autonomy.

Strategies and Policies Used by BRICS:

1. **Bilateral and Multilateral Diplomacy:** They collaborate on global issues through active diplomacy at both bilateral and multilateral levels, seeking to influence international organizations and global forums to promote their common interests.

2. **Diverse National Economies:** Each BRICS country has a unique economy and industrial base, and they seek to capitalize on these differences to promote economic complementarity within the group.

3. **Industrial and Commercial Policies:** They adopt industrial and commercial policies to promote economic growth and protect national strategic industries.

4. **Scientific and Technological Cooperation:** They collaborate in scientific research and technological development to stimulate innovation and compete globally.

5. **Strategic Investments:** They make strategic investments in key sectors such as infrastructure, energy, and advanced technologies to support economic growth and national security.

6. **Culture and Soft Power:** They use the promotion of culture and soft power to enhance their global image and positively influence global perceptions of themselves.

7. **Economic Diplomacy:** They actively participate in international economic and trade summits to promote trade and investments.

8. **Management of Natural Resources:** They adopt policies to strategically manage natural resources and ensure food and energy security.

9. **Sustainable Development:** They are committed to promoting sustainable development policies to address environmental and social challenges.

In an increasingly interconnected world, the BRICS face evolving challenges and opportunities. Their ability to effectively balance globalization with their national needs will be crucial to their success and role in the emerging world order. By maintaining a flexible and adaptable approach, these countries can continue to leverage their economic growth and geopolitical influence to shape the future of the world.

17. Human Rights • Analysis of the Human Rights Situation in BRICS Countries:

1. **Brazil:** In the context of Brazil, the human rights situation has been influenced by challenges such as urban violence, especially in favelas. Security forces have often been criticized for the excessive use of force. Racial discrimination and violence against minorities, including Indigenous peoples, remain persistent concerns. However, the country has made progress in strengthening women's rights and combating impunity for human rights crimes.

2. **Russia:** In Russia, human rights organizations often report restrictions on freedom of press and expression. Laws regarding homosexual propaganda have raised concerns about LGBTQ+ rights. The situation of ethnic minorities, such as Chechens, has been a subject of international debate.

3. **India:** India is a diverse country with complex human rights-related challenges. Caste-based discrimination persists, and religious tensions

have been a growing concern. However, the country has made significant progress in promoting education and addressing extreme poverty.

4. **China:** China has attracted international attention for its human rights situation. The suppression of protests in Tibet and the handling of the rights of ethnic minorities like the Uighurs have raised global concerns. Online censorship and media control are well-known issues, and political dissidents may face persecution.

5. **South Africa:** South Africa has a history of human rights struggles, emerging from apartheid. The country has made progress in promoting minority rights but still faces challenges related to economic inequality and crime.

It's important to note that the human rights situation is complex and multifaceted in each of these BRICS countries. Each nation has made progress in some areas but faces challenges in others. Furthermore, the perception of human rights may vary depending on cultural and political perspectives.

The BRICS often seek to balance the promotion of human rights with national sovereignty. This can lead to differing positions in international forums. However, the promotion of human rights remains an important topic in global discussions, and the human rights situation in BRICS countries continues to be a subject of international attention and debate.

6. **Brazil:** In the context of Brazil, the human rights situation has been influenced by challenges such as urban violence, especially in favelas. Security forces have often been criticized for the excessive use of force. Racial discrimination and violence against minorities, including Indigenous peoples, are persistent concerns. However, the country has made progress in strengthening women's rights and combating impunity for human rights crimes.

7. **Russia:** In Russia, human rights organizations often report restrictions on freedom of press and expression. Laws regarding homosexual propaganda have raised concerns about LGBTQ+ rights. The situation of ethnic minorities, such as Chechens, has been a subject of international debate.

8. **India:** India is a diverse country with complex human rights-related challenges. Caste-based discrimination persists, and religious tensions have been a growing concern. However, the country has made significant progress in

promoting education and addressing extreme poverty.

9. **China:** China has attracted international attention for its human rights situation. The suppression of protests in Tibet and the handling of the rights of ethnic minorities like the Uighurs have raised global concerns. Online censorship and media control are well-known issues, and political dissidents may face persecution.

10. **South Africa:** South Africa has a history of human rights struggles, having emerged from apartheid. However, the country still faces challenges related to economic inequality and crime. The South African government has worked to promote minority rights and address gender issues.

Each BRICS country has a unique human rights situation, with a set of challenges and progress. The perception of human rights can vary widely both within and outside these countries. Additionally, it's important to emphasize that the human rights situation is constantly evolving, with recent developments having a significant impact on global perception.

The BRICS often face challenges when balancing the promotion of human rights with their needs for national sovereignty. However, the human rights theme remains an important part of global discussions and continues to be a subject of international attention and debate.

11. **Brazil:** In the Brazilian context, human rights violations are often associated with violence in favelas, where police operations can lead to human rights abuses. Discrimination against minorities, including Indigenous peoples and the Black population, is a persistent issue. Over the years, Brazil has also grappled with challenges related to women's safety and domestic violence, but it has made progress in implementing laws to protect victims.

12. **Russia:** In Russia, human rights organizations frequently report limitations on freedom of expression and the repression of dissenting voices. The situation of minorities, including LGBTQ+ individuals, is subject to legal and social restrictions. Political protests can be suppressed, and activists may face intimidation and arrests.

13. **India:** India is a diverse nation with a rich cultural diversity but also a history of caste discrimination and religious tensions. Violence against women has been a significant concern, with incidents of rape and domestic violence sparking public outrage. The country is working

on legal and social reforms to address these challenges.

14. **China:** China has garnered increasing international attention for its handling of human rights. The suppression of protests in Tibet and concerns regarding the rights of ethnic minorities like the Uighurs have been widely reported. Online and media censorship is prevalent, and political dissidents can face severe consequences.

15. **South Africa:** South Africa has a history of human rights struggles, with the end of apartheid as a turning point. However, the country still faces challenges related to economic inequality and crime. Land issues and agrarian reform have been a source of tension as the South African government seeks to address extreme poverty.

Each BRICS country has a unique human rights situation, with specific challenges and progress. The perception of human rights can vary widely, and both internal and international debates continue to play a significant role. The human rights situation is in constant flux, with recent developments potentially having a significant impact on global perception and national policies.

16. **Brazil:** In the Brazilian context, the human rights situation has also been influenced by a series of environmental issues. The deforestation

of the Amazon and the destruction of natural habitats have raised global concerns as they threaten the lives of Indigenous populations and contribute to climate change. The management of natural resources and the protection of the rights of Indigenous communities have become central issues in the human rights discourse in Brazil.

17. **Russia:** Russia has witnessed the consolidation of centralized power and the restriction of freedom of the press and expression in recent years. Human rights organizations have documented cases of arbitrary arrests of political opponents and activists. Furthermore, the situation of sexual minorities, such as LGBTQ+ individuals, has been challenging, with laws against "homosexual propaganda" limiting freedom of expression and access to support services.

18. **India:** India has made significant progress in education and poverty alleviation but continues to face challenges in promoting women's rights and preventing gender-based violence. Additionally, religious tensions and intercommunity violence have been a growing concern in recent years. Caste-based discrimination persists, although the government has enacted laws to promote equality.

19. **China:** China has garnered increasing international attention for its handling of human rights, with concerns about the repression of critical voices and the situation of ethnic minorities. Mass surveillance, including online communications monitoring and facial recognition, has become a significant issue related to privacy and personal freedom. The situation of ethnic minorities, particularly the Uighurs, has drawn international attention, with allegations of mass detentions and human rights violations.

20. **South Africa:** South Africa continues to grapple with economic and social inequality issues inherited from the apartheid era. While the country has made progress in improving equality and social justice, there is still much work to be done. Land and agrarian reform have been topics of debate and tension. However, South Africa remains an example of a peaceful transition from racial segregation to a multiracial democracy.

In each of these BRICS countries, the human rights situation is influenced by a unique set of factors. Challenges and progress vary widely, and the perception of human rights can be subjective and influenced by cultural and political variables. The promotion and protection of human rights remain important topics of international debate, with many organizations and governments working to address ongoing challenges and seek solutions to improve the human rights situation worldwide.

21. **Brazil:** In the Brazilian context, the human rights situation has also been influenced by police violence, especially in the favelas of major cities. Numerous cases of abuse and homicides committed by police forces have raised questions about the lack of accountability and transparency in investigations. Additionally, threats and attacks against human rights defenders are concerning and pose challenges to freedom of expression and association.

22. **Russia:** In recent years, Russia has seen an increase in restrictions on freedom of the press and expression. Laws limiting the activities of foreign non-governmental organizations (NGOs) have made it difficult for human rights activists to work. The situation of sexual minorities, including LGBTQ+ individuals, has become more difficult due to anti-gay propaganda laws and social discrimination.

23. **India:** India is a country characterized by extraordinary cultural diversity but faces human rights challenges, including caste discrimination and religious tensions. Increasing political

polarization has led to an environment where critical voices are often suppressed or threatened. Nevertheless, the country has made progress in promoting education and access to healthcare.

24. **China:** China has attracted international attention for its handling of human rights, particularly for the situation of ethnic minorities like the Uighurs in the Xinjiang region. There have been allegations of mass detentions, forced labor, and other human rights violations. Online censorship is widespread, and restrictions on freedom of expression are notable. However, China is also a major player in poverty alleviation and has achieved significant economic progress.

25. **South Africa:** South Africa has been an example of a peaceful transition from a system of racial segregation to a multiracial democracy. However, the country still faces challenges related to economic and social inequality, with an unequal distribution of resources and opportunities. The issue of land and agrarian reform has been a source of tension as the government seeks to address issues of social justice and economic development.

The human rights situation is complex in each of these BRICS countries and is influenced by a range of factors. Challenges and progress vary significantly, and the perception of human rights can vary depending on cultural and political perspectives. The promotion and protection of human rights remain a priority globally, with many organizations and governments working to address these challenges and striving for greater justice and equality worldwide.

In conclusion, the human rights situation in BRICS countries is complex and varied, with each country facing unique challenges and opportunities. As these emerging countries continue to play an increasingly significant role on the global stage, it is crucial to closely monitor the human rights situation in each country and effectively address critical issues. Transparency, accountability, and open dialogue are key tools in addressing human rights issues and working toward sustainable solutions. While BRICS countries continue to have a significant impact on global politics and economics, the issue of human rights remains a crucial part of the global debate on justice and equality.

18. Future of BRICS: Prospects and Future Challenges for BRICS in the New World Order.

BRICS, consisting of Brazil, Russia, India, China, and South Africa, have emerged as a significant force in the context of the new world order. However, they face a range of prospects and challenges in their future path:

Future Prospects:

1. **Economic Power:** BRICS countries continue to grow economically and exert greater influence in international organizations like the G20. China, in particular, has become a dominant economic power.

2. **Cooperation:** BRICS have the potential to strengthen economic and political cooperation among themselves, which could lead to greater global stability.

3. **Reform of Global Institutions:** These countries have sought reform of international financial institutions like the International Monetary Fund (IMF) to better reflect the changing global power balance.

4. **Innovation and Technology:** Some BRICS members, such as China and India, are at the forefront of technological development and

innovation and can contribute to shaping global technological evolution.

5. **Economic Integration:** There are opportunities for further economic integration among these countries, such as intra-BRICS trade and collaboration in key sectors like energy and infrastructure.

Future Challenges:

1. **Political Differences:** BRICS have political divergences and national objectives that can make cooperation on global issues challenging. For example, China and India have had territorial tensions and geopolitical rivalries.

2. **Sustainable Development:** Addressing environmental issues and promoting sustainable development is a significant challenge, especially considering the massive environmental impact of some BRICS economies.

3. **Human Rights:** The human rights situation in some BRICS countries has been a matter of international concern and could pose an obstacle to their global reputation.

4. **Economic Instability:** BRICS economies are susceptible to economic instability, such as

financial crises or fluctuations in commodity prices, which could undermine their growth.

5. **Global Competition:** BRICS must navigate a world characterized by increasing geopolitical rivalries, including competition between the United States and China.

The future of BRICS will depend on their ability to overcome these challenges and capitalize on emerging opportunities. Cooperation among these countries on global issues, along with deepening economic integration and collaboration in key sectors, could significantly shape the new world order. However, addressing political differences and working together to tackle global challenges characteristic of the 21st century will be crucial.

Certainly, let's further explore the prospects and future challenges for BRICS in the new world order:

Additional Future Prospects:

6. **Role in International Organizations:** BRICS seek to play a more influential role in organizations like the G20, IMF, and World Bank. They can work together to reform these institutions to better reflect the current economic and political reality.

7. **Infrastructure Investments:** Infrastructure is a key element of economic development. BRICS can collaborate to promote joint infrastructure projects, improving connectivity among them and contributing to regional integration.

8. **Scientific and Technological Cooperation:** Research and technological development are essential for economic innovation. BRICS can collaborate on scientific research, the development of advanced technologies, and addressing global challenges such as public health and climate change.

9. **Promotion of Trade and Investment:** BRICS can work to simplify trade procedures and promote investments among themselves, enhancing the flow of goods and services and contributing to economic growth.

Additional Future Challenges:

6. **Geopolitical Tensions:** Geopolitical tensions among some BRICS members, like China and India, can hinder cooperation. Peaceful resolution of conflicts and dialogue will be essential to avoid damaging escalation.

7. **Cybersecurity and Defense:** With the increasing importance of technology and

cybersecurity, BRICS must address the challenges of cybersecurity and defense, protecting critical infrastructure and sensitive information.

8. **Environmental Sustainability:** The environmental impact of BRICS economies is significant. They should collaborate to address climate change, promote clean energy, and protect vital resources like water.

9. **Human Rights and Freedoms:** The human rights situation in some BRICS countries remains a concern. To gain a better global reputation, they must address human rights issues transparently and responsibly.

10. **Economic Vulnerability:** BRICS economies may be vulnerable to global economic shocks. They should take measures to reduce their reliance on commodities and promote sustainable economic diversification.

The future of BRICS will be defined by their ability to address these challenges collaboratively and leverage emerging opportunities. Their influence on the international stage continues to grow, and their ability to cooperate on crucial global issues will be fundamental in shaping the future of the new world order.

Future Prospects:

10. **Addressing Inequality:** BRICS have growing economies but also face significant internal inequalities. To ensure sustainable and inclusive growth, they will need to adopt policies to reduce economic and social inequality, ensuring that the benefits of growth are widely distributed.

11. **Public Health:** The COVID-19 pandemic has highlighted the importance of public health and international health cooperation. BRICS can collaborate to strengthen their healthcare infrastructure and promote joint medical research to address future pandemic-related challenges.

12. **Education and Skilled Workforce:** Investing in education and developing a highly skilled workforce is crucial for long-term economic competitiveness. BRICS can develop joint education programs and academic exchanges to promote the training of qualified human resources.

13. **Promoting Peace and Security:** Geopolitical stability is essential for economic growth and development. BRICS can work together to

address regional tensions and promote peace through dialogue and diplomacy.

14. **Economic Diversification:** Reducing dependence on commodities and promoting diversified economic sectors will make BRICS economies less vulnerable to fluctuations in commodity prices and global financial crises.

Future Challenges:

11. **Geopolitical Rivalries:** Geopolitical tensions among BRICS, such as territorial disputes between China and India, can erode group cohesion. Managing these rivalries peacefully will be essential for the bloc's future.

12. **Environment and Climate Change:** BRICS economies are among the world's largest greenhouse gas emitters. Addressing climate change requires concrete commitments to emissions reduction and the adoption of renewable energy sources.

13. **Cybersecurity:** In the digital age, cybersecurity is a growing concern. BRICS will need to develop joint policies and protocols to address cyber threats.

14. **Human Rights:** Improving the human rights situation remains a critical challenge for some

BRICS countries, with concerns related to freedom of the press, judicial independence, and freedom of expression.

15. **Global Economic Instability:** BRICS will need to address the consequences of global economic instability, such as commodity price fluctuations and financial market volatility.

The future of BRICS presents a field of challenges and opportunities. How these countries address these challenges and work together to harness emerging opportunities will determine their role in shaping the new world order and the well-being of their populations. Cooperation among BRICS remains crucial for addressing complex global issues and contributing to greater global stability and prosperity.

Additional Future Prospects:

16. **Economic Diplomacy:** BRICS can intensify efforts in economic diplomacy by negotiating bilateral and multilateral trade agreements that promote trade and investment. Diversifying trade relationships will enhance economic resilience.

17. **Renewable Energy:** Adopting renewable energy sources is essential for addressing climate change. BRICS, with their vast energy resources, can collaborate in the development and dissemination of clean energy technologies.

18.   **Infrastructure Connectivity:**
Improving infrastructure connectivity among
BRICS countries would facilitate trade and
exchanges, as well as economic cooperation.
Projects like China's Belt and Road Initiative
(BRI) offer shared infrastructure development
opportunities.

19. **Active Participation:** BRICS can play a more
active role in resolving regional and global crises,
promoting diplomacy, and seeking peaceful
solutions to conflicts and tensions.

20.   **Scientific and Technological
Collaboration:** Joint research and
technological development are crucial for
innovation and global competitiveness. BRICS
can establish joint programs to promote science
and technology.

Additional Future Challenges:

16. **Global Trade Tensions:** BRICS have been
affected by global trade tensions, such as those
between the United States and China. They must
seek ways to mitigate negative impacts on
economies and markets.

17. **Economic Fragility:** Some BRICS economies
are vulnerable to economic shocks. Improving

financial stability and reducing excessive debt are essential to mitigate these risks.

18. **Addressing Protectionism:** Growing protectionism in many parts of the world presents a challenge for BRICS, which rely on international trade. They should support a rules-based multilateral trading system.

19. **Reform of Global Institutions:** Reforming international institutions remains a challenge, with political obstacles to overcome in achieving adequate representation in global forums.

20. **Technological Challenges:** BRICS will need to address emerging technological challenges such as cybersecurity, data protection, and artificial intelligence governance.

The future of BRICS is dynamic and uncertain, but these nations have demonstrated their resilience and commitment to influencing the global context. By continuing to work together on economic, political, and environmental issues, BRICS can play a significant role in shaping the future world order. Multilateral cooperation and dialogue remain crucial for addressing common challenges and capitalizing on emerging opportunities.

Future Prospects:

21. Space Collaboration: BRICS can expand their cooperation in space exploration, including sharing satellite technologies and conducting joint space missions for scientific and Earth observation purposes.

22. Strengthening Cultural Ties: Promoting cultural exchange among BRICS countries can contribute to better mutual understanding and foster tolerance. This can be achieved through student exchange programs, cultural festivals, and artistic collaborations.

23. Promoting Social Innovation: BRICS can collaborate to address social challenges through social innovation, promoting projects that improve access to healthcare, education, and well-being for disadvantaged communities.

24. Women's Participation: Empowering women and promoting female participation in politics and the economy can be shared goals among BRICS members, with policies to address gender inequalities.

Future Challenges:

21. Political Instability: Political instability in some BRICS members can hinder their cohesion. Maintaining open dialogue and seeking diplomatic solutions to internal and external political tensions is essential.

22. Access to Resources: BRICS share competition for natural resources in a growing world. Sustainable resource management will be a crucial challenge.

23. Human Rights Compliance: Human rights concerns persist in some BRICS countries. Addressing these issues transparently is fundamental for the group's legitimacy and credibility.

24. Regional Conflicts: BRICS are involved in various regional conflict situations. Peaceful conflict resolution and support for diplomatic solutions remain a challenge.

25. Adapting to Global Change: BRICS will need to adapt to a rapidly changing world where the balance of power can shift quickly. Flexibility and adaptability will be crucial.

The future of BRICS is a dynamic path, and their ability to collaborate and address complex challenges will be crucial for their success. The diversity of BRICS members also offers a unique opportunity to tackle a wide range of global issues. Their influence continues to grow, and as a group, they can play a significant role in shaping the new world order, promoting stability, prosperity, and global cooperation.

In conclusion, BRICS (Brazil, Russia, India, China, and South Africa) represent a coalition of emerging nations that have gained significant influence in the global landscape. In the context of the evolving new world order, BRICS face a range of prospects and challenges that shape their future.

The future prospects for BRICS include the possibility of:

1. **Promoting Multilateral Cooperation:** BRICS can play a key role in promoting multilateral cooperation and strengthening global institutions to address challenges such as climate change, cybersecurity, and public health.

2. **Sustainable Economic Growth:** With a commitment to prudent economic policies and innovation, BRICS can maintain robust economic growth and contribute to global economic stability.

3. **Technological Innovation:** Collaboration among BRICS members can foster technological innovation and promote high-growth sectors such as artificial intelligence and biotechnology.

4. **Active Diplomacy:** BRICS can continue to play an active role in global diplomacy, seeking peaceful solutions to regional and global conflicts.

However, there are also significant challenges that BRICS must address, including:

1. **Geopolitical Tensions:** Tensions among some BRICS members, such as China and India, can undermine group cohesion and require diplomatic management.

2. **Climate Change:** BRICS are among the largest greenhouse gas emitters and must respond to pressures to reduce emissions and adopt clean energy sources.

3. **Human Rights:** Concerns about human rights in some BRICS countries require attention, with a need to improve human rights conditions to ensure the group's legitimacy.

4. **Global Economic Instability:** BRICS must be prepared to deal with global economic instability, including fluctuations in commodity prices and financial crises.

5. **Technological Challenges:** Cybersecurity and the governance of emerging technologies pose growing challenges that require coordinated actions.

Ultimately, the future of BRICS is a field of possibilities and challenges. How these countries address these challenges and work together to seize opportunities will be crucial for their role in shaping the new world order. Multilateral cooperation and dialogue remain essential for addressing complex global issues and contributing to greater global stability and prosperity.

19. Case Studies: Analyzing Specific Cases Related to BRICS

Certainly, let's examine some specific case studies related to BRICS to gain a deeper understanding of how these nations act and interact in the global context:

Case Study 1: The BRICS Bank (New Development Bank - NDB) The BRICS Bank, headquartered in Shanghai, was established to finance sustainable and infrastructural development projects in BRICS member countries and other emerging economies. It serves as an example of economic cooperation within BRICS.

- **Objectives:** The NDB aims to promote sustainable development by funding infrastructural, environmental, and social projects in BRICS member countries and beyond.

- **Successes:** The NDB has financed significant projects such as road construction in India, energy projects in China, and water management in South Africa. It also played a significant role during the COVID-19 pandemic by providing funding to address the health and economic crisis.

- **Challenges:** The NDB faces challenges such as fundraising, resource management, and coordination among member countries with diverse development priorities.

Case Study 2: China's Belt and Road Initiative (BRI) The BRI is an ambitious infrastructure and economic development program promoted by China, involving many countries, including some BRICS members.

- **Objectives:** The BRI aims to create a network of trade links and infrastructure connecting China to Europe, Africa, and Asia. This project has been seen as an opportunity for China to expand its economic and political influence.

- **Impact on BRICS:** Many BRICS countries, including Russia and India, are involved in the BRI. This has led to increased regional trade and investments but has also raised concerns about sovereignty and economic dependence.

- **Challenges:** The BRI has faced criticism regarding transparency, environmental sustainability, and governance. Balancing economic benefits with security concerns is an ongoing challenge.

Case Study 3: Cooperation in Energy and Agriculture Sectors BRICS countries also collaborate in key sectors such as energy and agriculture.

- **Energy:** Energy cooperation among BRICS includes technology sharing and the creation of cooperation platforms. For example, China and Russia have entered into energy agreements, while Brazil has collaborated with India on biofuels development.

- **Agriculture:** BRICS work together to address global food challenges. Brazil, for instance, is a major agricultural exporter, and India has a growing agricultural sector. Cooperation in this sector can contribute to global food security.

These case studies highlight the variety of sectors in which BRICS collaborate and the associated challenges and opportunities. Cooperation among BRICS is complex and evolving, but it remains an important component of the global geopolitical and economic landscape.

Case Study 4: Cooperation in Science and Research BRICS also collaborate in the fields of science and technology to promote innovation and development. This cooperation contributes to advancing knowledge and accelerating technological development.

- **Academic Exchange:** BRICS promote the exchange of students, researchers, and academics among their member countries. This fosters cultural diversity and contributes to the expansion of knowledge.

- **Joint Research:** BRICS countries collaborate on joint research projects on scientific and technological issues of common interest. This can range from renewable energy to medicine, artificial intelligence to astronomy.

- **Investment in Research and Development:** Some BRICS countries invest in research and development infrastructure, promoting technological innovation and global competitiveness.

Case Study 5: Military Cooperation BRICS maintain military relations and conduct joint exercises. Although military cooperation is not a primary objective of BRICS, it represents an aspect of their collaboration.

- **Joint Exercises:** BRICS have conducted joint military exercises, such as anti-terrorism exercises like "Peace Mission" and naval exercises. These exercises promote cooperation among the armed forces of member countries.

- **Sharing Military Techniques:** BRICS countries can share experiences and military techniques to enhance their defense capabilities and participate in United Nations peacekeeping operations.

- **Common Security Challenges:** BRICS can collaborate to address common security challenges, such as international terrorism and maritime piracy.

Case Study 6: Monetary Diplomacy BRICS have also explored opportunities for collaboration in the financial and monetary sector.

- **Resolution of Currency Conflicts:** During the global financial crisis of 2008, BRICS sought to coordinate monetary policies to mitigate the crisis's effects on their countries.

- **BRICS Bank:** As mentioned earlier, the creation of the BRICS Bank aims to provide funding for infrastructural projects in member countries. This represents a significant effort in financial cooperation.

- **Reforming the IMF:** BRICS have supported the reform of international financial institutions, such as the International Monetary Fund, to better reflect current economic and political realities.

These case studies demonstrate the diversity of areas in which BRICS seek to collaborate, from the scientific and technological field to the military and financial sectors. Their cooperation is motivated by the pursuit of common solutions to global challenges and the goal of promoting stability and economic growth in their member countries and beyond.

Case Study 7: Cooperation in the Renewable Energy Sector

BRICS recognize the importance of renewable energy in the transition to a more sustainable future. Some BRICS members are among the world's leading producers and consumers of energy, and cooperation in this sector can have a significant impact:

- **Solar Energy:** India and China, in particular, are making massive investments in solar technologies. Collaboration between these countries can contribute to the development and widespread adoption of affordable and efficient solar solutions.

- **Wind Energy:** Some BRICS countries, such as Brazil and South Africa, have harnessed wind resources for energy production. Sharing best practices and technologies can further stimulate the adoption of wind energy.

- **Green Technologies:** Joint research and development of green technologies, such as high-capacity batteries or energy storage systems, can help mitigate climate change and promote energy independence.

Case Study 8: Cultural and Academic Cooperation BRICS are characterized by diverse cultures and traditions. Cultural and academic cooperation is essential for promoting mutual understanding and intercultural dialogue:

- **Cultural Exchanges:** BRICS organize cultural festivals, art exhibitions, and culinary events to share their cultural diversity. These events raise awareness and promote mutual interest.

- **Academic Collaboration:** Universities in BRICS countries promote academic exchanges and research collaborations. This fosters the development of new knowledge and technologies.

- **Language Promotion:** Promoting the languages of BRICS countries, such as

Portuguese, Russian, and Hindi, can facilitate communication and trade among members.

Case Study 9: Space Cooperation Space exploration is a sector in which some BRICS members have demonstrated expertise. Space cooperation can lead to shared benefits:

- **Shared Satellites:** India has launched satellites for other BRICS countries, showcasing its technological prowess in space. This collaboration can improve satellite coverage and connectivity in the involved regions.

- **Space Research:** Cooperation in space research can include joint missions to explore the Moon or Mars and the sharing of scientific data.

- **Terrestrial Applications:** Technologies developed for space exploration can have terrestrial applications, such as weather forecasting, natural resource management, and communication.

These case studies further illustrate how BRICS seek to collaborate in various sectors to promote sustainable economic growth, technological innovation, and international cooperation. The diversity of skills and resources among BRICS members offers many opportunities for shared development and the achievement of common goals.

Conclusion In the conclusion, we consider the role of BRICS in the new world order and some possible future scenarios:

BRICS, composed of Brazil, Russia, India, China, and South Africa, represent a group of emerging nations with significant economic and political potential. Their cooperation aims to challenge Western hegemony and contribute to shaping a fairer and multipolar new world order.

The role of BRICS in the global economy is remarkable. China has become the world's second-largest economy, and India is steadily growing. These countries significantly contribute to global economic growth and are promoting regional trade agreements and infrastructure development initiatives that can have a long-term impact.

BRICS are also seeking to influence international financial institutions such as the International Monetary Fund (IMF) and the World Bank to better reflect current economic realities and reduce dependence on Western institutions.

In the political arena, BRICS face challenges and opportunities. There are differences among members on political and strategic issues, but also a common willingness to promote global stability and peace.

However, the future of BRICS is not without obstacles. Tensions among members, cultural differences, and internal challenges can limit their ability to cooperate effectively. Additionally, the evolving geopolitical context, with growing rivalries among global powers, can test the cohesion of BRICS.

Possible Future Scenarios Include:

1. **Strengthening Cooperation:** BRICS could strengthen their economic, political, and strategic cooperation, expanding their impact in the new world order and contributing to global stability.

2. **Internal Challenges:** Tensions among members could escalate, leading to reduced cohesion within the group. This could weaken their ability to influence the new world order.

3. **Deepening Bilateral Relations:** Some BRICS members might focus more on developing their bilateral relations with global powers like the United States or the European Union, diverting attention away from intra-group cooperation.

In Conclusion, BRICS have the potential to play a significant role in the new world order, but internal and external challenges may influence their future path. Their ability to navigate these

challenges and capitalize on opportunities will largely determine their impact on global changes in the decades to come.

Continuation of Future Perspectives: 4. Economic Integration: BRICS could seek to deepen economic integration among themselves, promoting mutual trade and investments. Eliminating trade barriers and standardizing trade norms could facilitate greater economic cooperation.

5. **Technological Advancement:** China, in particular, is making significant strides in technology, from artificial intelligence to 5G technology. BRICS could cooperate in research and technological development to compete globally in these key sectors.

6. **Reforming Global Institutions:** BRICS continue to support reform of international financial institutions such as the IMF and the World Bank. They could intensify efforts to gain greater representation and influence in these institutions.

7. **Defending International Norms:** BRICS may engage in defending international norms and multilateralism at a time when such principles are being tested by growing unilateral and nationalistic trends.

8. **Environmental Sustainability:** With increasing environmental concerns, BRICS may collaborate more closely in researching and developing sustainable technologies and combating climate change.

9. **Global Crisis Management:** BRICS could develop capabilities for managing global crises, such as responding to pandemics or natural disasters, demonstrating solidarity and intervention capacity.

10. **Promoting Peace and Security:** BRICS may seek to promote global peace and security through dialogue, preventive diplomacy, and cooperation in United Nations peacekeeping operations.

Deepening BRICS Dynamics: 11. **Sectoral Collaboration:** BRICS may seek to collaborate in specific sectors such as energy, agriculture, education, and healthcare. This sectoral cooperation could lead to tangible developments and tangible benefits for the citizens of member countries.

12. **Multi-Track Diplomacy:** BRICS could employ multi-track diplomacy approaches, involving not only governments but also civil society, businesses, and academic institutions to promote broader understanding and cooperation among member countries.

13. **Infrastructure Investments:** Increased commitment to funding and implementing large-scale infrastructure projects within and among BRICS countries could lead to improved transport networks, telecommunications, and energy access.

14. **Cultural Exchanges:** Promoting cultural exchanges among BRICS countries could contribute to better mutual understanding and cultural openness. This could include cultural festivals, student exchange programs, and the promotion of languages and traditions of member countries.

15. **Language Promotion:** BRICS may consider adopting a common language or promoting the use of languages of member countries in trade and diplomatic relations to enhance communication and cooperation.

16. **Participation in Regional Organizations:** BRICS could seek to strengthen their presence and influence in regional organizations, such as the African Union or the Organization of American States, to extend their reach and enhance relations with other regions.

17. **Balancing National and Collective Interests:** BRICS face the challenge of balancing their national interests with collective

group interests. Finding a balance between national sovereignty and multilateral cooperation will remain a key challenge.

18. **Engagement in Global Conflict Resolution:** BRICS could play a more active role in global conflict resolution, acting as mediators or supporting diplomatic efforts in areas such as the Middle East, Africa, and Asia.

19. **Commitment to a Multipolar World:** BRICS support the idea of a multipolar world in which no single nation or bloc of nations dominates. They can work to promote a fairer and more inclusive international system.

20. **Monitoring and Evaluation:** BRICS could develop monitoring and evaluation mechanisms to measure the effectiveness of their initiatives and ensure they are achieving their goals.

BRICS, with their diversity and resources, continue to influence the global landscape. Their ability to adapt to emerging challenges and capitalize on opportunities will largely determine their impact on global politics and the evolution of the new world order.

Deepening BRICS Dynamics: 21. **Innovation Collaboration:** BRICS could intensify collaboration in innovation and scientific research. This could include the exchange of knowledge and advanced technologies in areas such as medicine, renewable energy technology, and artificial intelligence.

22. **Financial Market Cooperation:** BRICS may further develop their domestic financial markets and promote cooperation in the banking and financial sectors. This could involve opening branches of BRICS country financial institutions in their respective markets.

23. **Active Participation in Regional Organizations:** BRICS could increase their participation and influence in regional organizations such as ASEAN or Mercosur to promote greater economic and political cooperation in their respective regions.

24. **Promotion of Human Rights:** BRICS may commit to improving the human rights situation in their respective countries and promoting higher global standards in this area, demonstrating leadership in human rights compliance.

25. **Health Diplomacy:** Given experiences with epidemics like Ebola and the COVID-19 pandemic, BRICS could develop more effective health diplomacy to address global health

challenges and strengthen healthcare systems in member countries.

26.   **Arms Control Cooperation:** BRICS may seek to promote nuclear disarmament and greater transparency in arms proliferation, contributing to international stability.

27.   **Green Economy Growth:** The adoption of green economic growth strategies could be at the center of BRICS economic policies to address environmental challenges and promote sustainable development.

28.   **Cultural Integration:** Promoting cultural integration could involve creating cultural centers and artistic exchanges among member countries, contributing to greater mutual understanding of cultures.

29.   **Deepening Relations with Africa:** BRICS could intensify their cooperation with African countries, strengthening political, economic, and cultural relations and contributing to Africa's progress.

30.   **Collaboration in Artificial Intelligence and Cybersecurity:** Given the growing challenges in cybersecurity, BRICS could cooperate to address cyber threats and promote responsible use of artificial intelligence.

BRICS, through their cooperation and commitment, can significantly influence the global landscape. Their dedication to addressing common challenges and promoting multilateral cooperation will remain crucial in determining their role in the new world order.

In Conclusion, BRICS (Brazil, Russia, India, China, and South Africa) represent a group of emerging nations playing an increasingly relevant role in the context of the new world order. Dynamics within BRICS and their impact on the global stage are influenced by a complex set of factors.

These five nations have a diversity of interests, cultures, economies, and political systems, making their cooperation and achievement of common goals a dynamic and challenging process. However, BRICS have demonstrated the ability to work together on issues of shared interest, such as the reform of international financial institutions and the promotion of sustainable development.

BRICS have a significant impact on global economic policy. They have contributed to shifting the balance of economic power toward emerging economies and are becoming increasingly influential in international trade negotiations. The opening of their markets and the promotion of mutual investments have fostered trade and economic growth.

On the political front, BRICS have sought to play a constructive role in resolving global conflicts and promoting a fairer world order. However, they must confront challenges such as differences in their foreign policies and human rights issues.

In the field of innovation and technology, BRICS are becoming important hubs for research and development. Their collaboration in high-tech areas such as artificial intelligence and renewable energy is crucial for global progress.

BRICS also play a crucial role in promoting sustainable development and combating climate change. Sustainable policies adopted by group members can serve as examples for other nations.

In summary, the future of BRICS will be determined by their ability to balance national interests with collective ones, address emerging challenges such as technology and the environment, and play a constructive role in the context of the new world order. Cooperation within BRICS will continue to be crucial in addressing global challenges and promoting a multipolar and inclusive world.

In this work, we have explored in detail the role of BRICS in the context of the new world order.

BRICS, composed of Brazil, Russia, India, China, and South Africa, represent a group of emerging nations that are playing an increasingly relevant role on the global stage. We have examined several key aspects related to this topic, including:

1. **Introduction to BRICS:** We started with an overview of BRICS, defining them and outlining their history and evolution.

2. **BRICS Economies:** We examined in detail the economies of each member and their global impact, highlighting challenges and opportunities.

3. **BRICS Politics:** We looked at the internal and external policies of BRICS countries, including dynamics in their bilateral relationships.

4. **International Relations:** We analyzed BRICS' relations with other global actors, such as the United States, the European Union, and other regional groups.

5. **New World Order:** We defined the concept of the new world order and how BRICS are contributing to shaping it.

6. **BRICS' Impact on the New World Order:** We examined how BRICS influence global power

balance, economic policy, and geopolitical dynamics.

7. **Technology and Innovation:** We explored BRICS' role in technological development and innovation, including challenges and opportunities.

8. **Sustainable Development:** We examined the sustainable development policies and practices adopted by BRICS and their environmental impact.

9. **Inequalities and Disparities:** We looked at inequalities within and among BRICS countries and related challenges.

10. **Conflicts and Cooperation:** We analyzed conflicts and areas of cooperation among BRICS members.

11. **Climate Change:** We explored BRICS' role and responsibility in the context of climate change.

12. **Defense and Security Strategies:** We examined BRICS' defense and security policies in the new world order.

13. **Culture and Society:** We delved into the impact of BRICS' cultures and societies on the world.

14. **Financial Institutions:** We looked at the role of BRICS financial institutions, such as the BRICS Bank.

15. **International Trade:** We analyzed BRICS' role in international trade and economic implications.

16. **Globalization vs. Nationalism:** We discussed how BRICS balance globalization and nationalism.

17. **Human Rights:** We examined the human rights situation in BRICS countries.

18. **Future of BRICS:** We explored future prospects and challenges for BRICS in the new world order.

19. **Case Studies:** We conducted a detailed analysis of specific case studies related to BRICS.

20. **Conclusion:** Finally, we reflected on the role of BRICS in the new world order and possible future scenarios.

For further insights and resources, you can consult the websites of international organizations such as UNESCO, the International Monetary Fund (IMF), the World Trade Organization (WTO), and the official BRICS website. Additionally, books, academic articles, and research reports can be valuable sources for further exploring this fascinating topic. This book provides a comprehensive overview of BRICS and their dynamics while also inviting readers to continue exploring this captivating subject through additional resources.